# THE PROFESSORS OF TEACHING

*SUNY SERIES IN TEACHER PREPARATION
AND DEVELOPMENT
ALAN R. TOM, EDITOR*

# The Professors of Teaching

## AN INQUIRY

Richard Wisniewski
and Edward R. Ducharme
*Editors*

STATE UNIVERSITY OF NEW YORK PRESS

Published by
State University of New York Press, Albany

For information, address State University of New York
Press, State University Plaza, Albany, N.Y., 12246


**Library of Congress Cataloging-in-Publication Data**

The Professors of teaching : an inquiry / edited by Richard Wisniewski
    and Edward R. Ducharme ; in collaboration with Russell M. Agne . . .
    [et al.].
        p.    cm.—(SUNY series in teacher preparation and
development)
    Bibliography: p.
    Includes index.
    ISBN 0-88706-901-0.   ISBN 0-88706-902-9 (pbk.)
    1. Education—United States—Graduate work.   2. College teachers—
Training of—United States.   I. Wisniewski, Richard.
II. Ducharme, Edward R.   III. Agne, Russell M.   IV. Series.
LB2372.E3P76   1988
378'.12'02373—dc19                                             88-12655
                                                                   CIP


10 9 8 7 6 5 4 3 2

*To the professors who shaped our academic lives*

# CONTENTS

# ACKNOWLEDGMENT

Special thanks to Marie Whitley White. She persevered despite many assurances that she was typing the final draft.

# CONTRIBUTORS

RUSSELL M. AGNE, College of Education & Social Services, University of Vermont, Burlington, Vermont.

CLINTON B. ALLISON, College of Education, University of Tennessee, Knoxville, Tennessee.

BARBARA G. BURCH, College of Education, Memphis State University, Memphis, Tennessee.

EDWARD R. DUCHARME, College of Education & Social Services, University of Vermont, Burlington, Vermont.

HENDRICK D. GIDEONSE, College of Education, University of Cincinnati, Cincinnati, Ohio.

J. STEPHEN HAZLETT, School of Education, Indiana State University, Terre Haute, Indiana.

JAMES RATHS, College of Education & Social Services, University of Vermont, Burlington, Vermont (in collaboration with Lilian Katz, University of Illinois, Urbana-Champaign, and Amy McAninch, University of Illinois, Urbana-Champaign).

MILTON SCHWEBEL, Graduate School of Applied and Professional Psychology, Rutgers University, Piscataway, New Jersey.

RICHARD WISNIEWSKI, College of Education, University of Tennessee, Knoxville, Tennessee.

# INTRODUCTION

This is a book which will give no comfort either to the enemies of the education professoriate (whose bad-tempered criticisms are not supported by hard evidence), or to its members (who may have only a little time to set their rambling house in order). The heart of the problem of The Professors of Teaching lies in their origins. The overwhelming majority of them, as is demonstrated here, began their careers in the lower schools, acquired in them their professional habits of mind, enjoyed only limited opportunities for doctoral study. The themes of this collaborative volume run persistently through the chapters and interlock, but this remains one of the most pervasive and persuasive of them all.

The prescription for reform is embarrassingly simple, in that the embarrassment will fall upon those who fail to take it seriously. Somehow, and soon, attitudes and policies in schools, colleges, and departments of education (SCDEs) will have to change. The place within them of those who are Professors of Teaching—teacher educators, if you will, but with a particular emphasis—must be dignified. If the SCDEs of the 1990s are not professional schools for teachers, they will be nothing: no other future appears to be accessible to them. In the past, some among them have achieved a measure of academic visibility by contriving to transform themselves into places for the study disjointed from the research-based practice of education. Economists, historians, and sociologists—who have many profound things to say about educational phenomena—have duly won esteem for themselves and for the institutions they inhabit. But even this shortcut to full incorporation within the academy has proved to be a cul-de-sac.

As these authors see it, the trouble with the SCDEs is that there are too many of them and that they occupy too much territory. The professional origins of those who teach in them and the weakness of many of the institutional contexts conspire to sharpen the tension between academic and clinical cultures. These are severe in many fields (medicine or architecture, for example) but the special circumstances of teacher education raise such tensions above the point at which they can be accommodated. So much so that some of the writers here fleetingly wonder whether teacher education would not be safer at a distance from the academic hegemony, protected within autonomous institutions.

But that, of course, would be to replace one problem by another. It is, nevertheless, clear that if there are to be fewer SCDEs and if their mission must be that of a professional school for teachers, then within the University itself they need a greater degree of distinctness and autonomy than is currently enjoyed. For a foreign observer at least, one implication of such a requirement (touched upon lightly at several points in the following pages) is the progressive disentanglement of SCDEs from the Arts and Science web. It is dangerous to assume that members of Arts and Science departments can be professionally competent not only in imparting to undergraduates the subject matter appropriate to a higher education, but also in relating that subject matter to the pedagogy and curriculum of the elementary and secondary school. Such an assumption structurally inhibits the professors of teaching from making explicit precisely what it is that they are supposed to be professors of.

In a redefined position within the academic firmament—a position which, for the most part, can be redefined by them—the professors of teaching can then apply themselves to the research inherent in their role and not in conflict with it. The authors of this book are not prepared to leave such a challenge unanswered. For them, with characteristically differing emphases, the professors of teaching must abandon their neglect of or even contempt for research. Until they do, the rights of academic citizenship will be properly denied to them. That effort requires a shifting of priorities, and a sophisticated use of available time. People who do not think scholarship important will never find time to engage in it.

At the same time, and unless the baby is once again to disappear with the bathwater, such a shift must not be accompanied by a loss of the clinical context. Teacher education must, it is argued, be bicultural, and that means preserving or acquiring the capacity to render to the schools an appropriate service based upon academic expertise. If Universities can only do (better or worse) that which other professional agencies can also do (more or less expensively), then there is little reason for them to remain in serious business. That, precisely, is why the three essential characteristics of the effective professors of teaching—the training of teachers, research, service—must be integrated. As long as they are perceived as being in opposition, each of them will of necessity be ill-performed.

This conclusion explains and justifies the repeated emphasis in all the chapters of this book upon the imperiousness of the research agenda. The words of the authors record and reflect a wealth of experience of SCDEs in which the teacher trainers count themselves too busy to engage in research, and the researchers consider themselves too grand to meddle in the business of making better teachers. The necessary conditions for ending that perilous schism are described, although not listed. That is why I have attempted, in a way which is perhaps arbitrary, to distill them here in the introduction. They are: a reduction in the number of SCDEs, a celebration of their mission as educators of teachers, an integration of research with their teaching and service functions, a greater measure of institutional identity, the strengthening of the clinical contexts in which they must work.

These I read as common prescriptions or axioms in the following chapters. Each of them requires a coalition for change, inside even more than outside SCDEs. There is, however, one such change which lies unambiguously within the territorial powers of SCDEs, and to which (I believe) only one reference is made in this volume. The multiplication and divisive power of departments within SCDEs is certain to astonish any foreign observer of them. This phenomenon appears to have few close analogies in other schools or sectors of the university. Doubtless, it has arisen for good historical reasons—the effort to specialize, to create subprofessional monopolies, even to divert attention from the unlovely business of educating teachers. But the reasons for the multiplication of departments are, when stood upon their heads, precisely the reasons for now reducing their number and their power. Teacher education is unlikely to prevail as the defining function of the SCDE when it is relegated to a department alongside or beneath many others with an apparently superior clientele and with a faculty sympathetic to the music of research (and with perhaps more time to enjoy or to write it).

This is a book about an American problem which only Americans could have written. A foreigner can and should do no more than attempt to summarize their conclusions and point to the importance of what has been well-argued. The problem in the United States may simply be more clear but not for that reason more real than it is in other developed countries. There is a sense, and not in the United

States alone, in which teacher education will shortly be one century old. The dominant notes of this book are of opportunity and of danger. The opportunity is there because the better education of teachers is, at last, widely recognized as a necessary component of effective reform in education. The danger is there because teacher education is institutionally weak and intellectually uncertain. The critical question is whether the enterprise of teacher education can reshape itself fast enough to meet the imminent challenge of having to produce better teachers in larger numbers. If it does not, and in my view along the lines well described in this book, a second chance is unlikely.

That opportunity, that danger and that critical question recur in different forms in other developed societies. This volume therefore should be read as a contribution not only to the rich debate within the United States, but also to reflection and policymaking in other countries. In some of them, the necessary work has hardly begun.

HARRY JUDGE
Oxford University

# Why Study the Education Professoriate? An Introduction

RICHARD WISNIEWSKI
EDWARD R. DUCHARME

## INTRODUCTION

In this book, we seek to unravel a complex phenomenon: the origins, preparation, aspirations, and performance of professors of education in the United States. All the writers are professors of education. We are among the professors of teaching we seek to understand.

The book began serendipitously. Two of our number issued an invitation to discuss the education professoriate during the 1984 American Association of Colleges for Teacher Education Conference. The session was scheduled on a free evening, a time when conferees usually desert the hotel. Nonetheless, several of the authors came to the meeting. We learned that we had been independently grappling with similar questions: Who becomes a professor of education? Are we different from professors in other disciplines? What are the productivity levels of education professors? To what degree are professors responding to the educational reform movement? Were our individual perceptions of our peers unique? Our discussion confirmed: (1) we had a range of experiences, data, and ideas that we wished to probe; and (2) we believed that a deeper understanding of the professoriate would help us in our work and be of interest to colleagues.

Over the next two years, we met at the American Educational Research Association and the American Association of Colleges for Teacher Education conferences. We retreated for intensive weekend discussions in Tennessee, Ohio, Vermont, and New Jersey. There were many exchanges by phone and letter; we circulated drafts of papers. The idea of writing a book gradually emerged. We are indebted to our universities for supporting us in these endeavors.

It is difficult to identify precisely the origin of ideas among us. We frequently argued alternative explanations for the behaviors, status, and potential of our calling. We enjoyed the give-and-take of intellectual stimulation, of seldom having our first statement of an issue go unchallenged. Some ideas were lost in the process; others were strengthened as the group shaped its thoughts. The experience was stimulating as we discovered that we shared similar concerns about our calling.

We learned from one another. We heard viewpoints that we had not considered before, and we occasionally had to give up favorite ideas. Reality as viewed by some was seen as stereotypical thinking by others. As a result, we all do not agree on every idea presented in this book, but we are comfortable with its central themes. A happy part of this undertaking was the sense of camaraderie generated. The experience has had an impact on our understanding of ourselves, our colleagues, and our profession. We engaged in a seminar in the best sense of the term, building on our common and differentiated experiences as participant-observers in the world of teacher education. We challenged one another's views; we invite colleagues to do the same.


## OUR CONCERNS

We question the degree to which education professors want to strengthen their profession. In light of the growing demand that schools of education be reformed, this is a critical issue. Discomforted by the increasing professional distance separating many professors from the teachers they prepare, we are convinced that professors of education must become far more intensively involved in the educational reform movement and with the practicing profession. Simultaneously, we believe that we need to maintain the sense of perspective essential to professorial research. Our group grappled frequently with this major cleavage within the educational professoriate: the split between demands for service and scholarship. Clark (1987) expresses the point forcefully:

> A similar tension, we note in passing, is found in schools of education that must constantly attempt to become more scholarly in order to achieve and maintain legitimacy in the university family, while also involving themselves directly in improving educational practice. The first means research and publication; the second means time spent in the teacher education laboratory, the university elementary "lab school," the local school district, or the office of the state superintendent of public education.
>
> Professional schools vacillate between these two poles. A school of education may have struggled relentlessly throughout the 1970s to become a place of serious research and scholarship, under a virtual mandate from the campus administration and the academic brethren, year by year, academic appointment by academic appointment, to be respectable according to the letters and science norms of the campus. But then, in the 1980s, its administration and faculty attempt to swing the character of the school toward practice under pressure to do something to improve schools (p. 95).

We believe both goals can be achieved.

We are concerned about the quality of our profession. Educators will remember the 1980s as a decade when questions regarding the quality of public education attained national visibility. Two interrelated ideas focused attention on those responsible for teacher education: the belief that the quality of education is directly related to the quality of classroom teachers, and the realization that the quality of teachers is directly related to their preparation for teaching. A rigorous examination of the quality of teacher preparation requires an assessment of those whom we have dubbed the professors of teaching.

Questions about education programs are not new, but the intensity of criticism escalated in the 1980s. Arthur Bestor, James Conant, James Koerner, and others discussed teacher preparation in the

1950s and 1960s; they were critical of programs and of the faculty who taught the courses. During that era, efforts to improve teacher education introduced new curricula and program requirements. It was a time of expansion on most campuses, however, and insufficient attention was given to faculty quality, change, growth, and development. The experimental programs of the 1960s assumed that most teacher educators were capable of implementing new programs. The resistance of professors, the slowness of change and the power of traditional practices soon became apparent. During the 1970s and 1980s, declining enrollments and budgets, an aging faculty, rigid disciplinary barriers, and the growing social distance between professors and teachers further hampered innovation. Faculty development became a concern on many campuses.

As professors of education, we are deeply concerned with our fragmentation, scholarship, and unfulfilled potential. Our potential can be reached, but not without important changes in schools of education and in the behaviors of the education professoriate. The structure and ethos of our institutions, the roles and responsibilities of faculty must be dramatically altered over the coming decades. Only then can visions of reform such as those offered by the Holmes Group (1985), the Carnegie Forum (1986), and similar reports be realized.

Our central concern is with the utilization of the knowledge base available to teacher educators. We wonder if most professors are knowledgeable about current research in teacher education. Some argue that they know what is happening in the schools, apparently thinking that knowledge of practice suffices for the professoriate. Much recent research, including some in this book, demonstrates that the overwhelming majority of education professors were teachers and administrators at one time. We contend that the insights gained a number of years ago, but not regularly tested against research on schooling, teaching, and learning are grossly inadequate. Indeed, the formative experiences of the education professoriate as teachers and graduate students are both a strength and hindrance to examining education with fresh eyes.

Too many practices are viewed as "natural" or traditional and, hence, acceptable. Change in curricula or programs is impossible unless professors are serious students of their craft. Innovation also requires that those implementing changes alter their own behaviors. Is this a realistic expectation of professors of education? What is the potential for reform among those who prepare teachers and other educators? This book attempts to answer these questions.

Our common intellectual interest in understanding the professoriate coalesced us as a group, but we are also concerned with strengthening our calling. Each of us has been involved in efforts to improve the profession. It was in such activities that many of our perceptions were forged. We learned from attempts small and large to introduce new programs and to influence higher education, state, and even national policies. In addition to maintaining their professorial interests, all but one of the authors has served as a dean or a department head. Because these roles provide unique vantage points from which to assess faculties and programs, our perceptions are different and perhaps broader than if we had maintained career lines exclusively within the professorial role.

We have considered the impact our volume might have on the debate regarding the quality of schools of education and their professors. An honest assessment of any profession will reveal highs and lows. We would be unprofessional if we did not deal with weaknesses as well as strengths. We recognize that some critics may use our words to demean our profession, and we are discomforted by this prospect. As with all authors, we hope for a broad audience, but we recognize that most readers will be persons like ourselves— professors in the higher education community. We look forward to their reactions.

As we developed our work, we have been asked on occasion how what we are learning relates to the professoriate in other fields; for example, history, sociology, or business. Our work is not as comprehensive as that of Ladd and Lipset (1975) and Clark (1987) who studied the entire professoriate. The professoriate in other disciplines has not been one of our central concerns. Our goal was to learn what we could about professors of education. Perhaps in subsequent work, we or others may sharpen comparisons to other disciplines. For this to happen, however, there must be comparable studies of professors in other disciplines.

A reviewer of an early draft of this volume thought it presumptuous for a "secret" group to meet and produce a book sometimes denigrating the professoriate. Implicit in the remark was the view that we perceive ourselves superior to our peers. We disagree. We have the same origins as most professors of education. We believe our discussion is critical to the well-being of our profession. The issues discussed are vital to the future of the professoriate and of public education. We are indebted to predecessors who have raised similar issues over the years. These matters have concerned the best professors for generations. We believe these issues must now be debated in a forum more open than in the past.

Our goal is not to castigate colleagues, but to urge change and growth. We seek to understand ourselves as much as our peers. Convinced that reform in teacher education will be achieved only when the mainsprings of the educational establishment are fully understood, we demand more than superficial insights into our profession. The professors of teaching, the educational professoriate, are among the key mainsprings. We speak to their origins, behaviors, and potential.

## OUR MAIN THEMES

We are acutely aware of the difficulty of making statements that apply to all professors. While we may qualify our views too frequently, we recognize there are many factors that we could not possibly address. We realize how little is known about the professoriate because professionals seldom study themselves. We are indebted to a number of earlier writers, whom we gratefully acknowledge. Even so, the need for additional historical, descriptive, and ethnographic studies of the professoriate is clear.

We have attempted to reinforce selected themes in every chapter. This seeming redundancy is the result of our seeking consensus on what nine professors could mutually support. Among the themes:

- Research and scholarship are central to the academy and must be part of the lives of all professors of education.
- The continuing clash between public school and university cultures must be attenuated by scholarship derived from collaborative work with schools.
- The problem of defining the education professoriate is contextual and is aggravated by a virulent fragmentation.
- The education professoriate, while it has a unique image problem, is similar in most respects to professors in other disciplines.
- Schools of education must be reorganized or their potential cannot be reached.
- There is cause for cautious optimism regarding the future of the professors of teaching despite the enduring nature of their characteristics.

We believe these themes are substantiated by the literature, our individual and group analyses, and by the work of many colleagues.

The following chapters present a systematic inquiry into our calling. Each contribution is but a foray into the research and analysis that we hope will follow. There is little likelihood of large-scale resources for comprehensive research on the education professoriate. Further insights will probably derive from studies similar to those reported in this volume.

Stephen Hazlett opens our discussion with a review of the history of the education professoriate. He argues that we do not have a history, that our roots are fragmented and educators do not have the same sense of professional cohesiveness as persons in other disciplines. He cites Powell's study of Harvard's first professor of education, P. H. Hanus. Apparently Professor Hanus's experiences were not unique as other universities introduced departments of education at the turn of the century.

In the same vein, Clinton Allison describes the lives of three early professors of education at the University of Tennessee, men of modest education, high aspiration, and intense activity. Each college of education has similar persons in its history, professors who established the structure and traditions of teacher preparation. Readers will recognize in these biographies the ambiguities of existence among education professors persisting to this day. Hazlett and Allison make clear the need for a better sense of history and tradition among the education professoriate.

Milton Schwebel examines changing traditions and expectations in universities as they apply to professors of education. The renewed emphasis on research in the modern university clashes with practices in the education professoriate which have historically put a heavier premium on producing teachers rather than on generating knowledge.

Edward Ducharme and Russell Agne present data collected from approximately 1,200 professors of education in a national study. The information on the social class and educational origins of contemporary professors of education offers insights into the character of colleges of education, as well as their potential for change in an era of reform.

Barbara Burch adds to these insights with a survey of professors in and outside of colleges of education. She identifies some of the similarities and differences between the two. Debate regarding these variations dominated much of the give-and-take among the authors.

James Raths and his associates examine a fundamental tension in colleges of education: the split between clinical or field-oriented professors and those who adhere closely to the traditional academic and scholarly roles of the professoriate. While professors in many disciplines live in a world in which the cultures of the scientist and the practitioner produce a difficult plight, the problem appears especially acute for teacher educators.

Hendrik Gideonse examines the way a small sample of education professors spend their time through his analysis of logs kept by the group. Gideonse identifies tasks beyond teaching classes for which professors are responsible. His analysis reveals that how time is spent is a powerful indicator of the priority placed on various responsibilities, thereby revealing the ethos of an institution.

Richard Wisniewski discusses the characteristics of the ideal professor of education. He underscores that teaching and professional service must derive from a scholarly base.

The final chapter offers assertions regarding the future of schools of education. Some of the recommendations are not drawn explicitly from material in the preceding chapters, for example, the issue of extending preparation programs beyond the baccalaureate. We were not satisfied by producing a book which merely describes our calling. Indeed, our discussions sometimes drifted between two motivations: the desire to learn more about the professoriate and the desire to reform education in general and teacher preparation specifically. These two interests sometimes clashed, even while doing something as seemingly objective as discussing the lives of early professors.

A bibliography of works on the professoriate completes the book. We are indebted to many sources, but especially to several works published in the 1970s that stimulated our interest in the professoriate. These include the several articles edited by Bagley (1975) in a monograph issued by the Society of Professors of Education, Powell's work (1980) and the 74th Yearbook of the Society for the Scientific Study of Education edited by Ryan (1975). We are also indebted to Lortie's (1975) analysis of the teaching profession, which provides deep insights into the professional culture of which professors are merely a part. While our work was in progress, several other works have been published, indicating a growing interest in the professors of teaching. For example, Clark's already cited volume, Magrath and Egbert's volume (1987), the studies edited by Raths and Katz (1985), and the provocative insights offered by Judge (1982).

Finally, we recognize the tenuous nature of our book. We are, after all, professors of teaching, loyalists concerned about our profession. While we offer criticisms, we are no doubt blind to rationalizations implicit in our explanations. Despite our candor, our work is not an exposé. What would be revealed if schools of education and their professors were studied by ethnographers and others not immersed in the field? Hopefully, such studies will one day be available. Until then, we see our efforts as being in keeping with Morgan's (1983) book on diverse approaches to social science research. His concluding chapter is titled "In Research, As In Conversations, We Meet Ourselves." While our conversations are tangential to Morgan's methodological issues, his closing lines apply to our inquiry:

> . . . The position I am offering here does not seek to offer a point of view that will satisfy everyone. Rather, it seeks to present a position that we will be able to criticize and refine, perhaps in a way that takes us beyond conversation (p. 407).

Our hope is that our observations and advocacies encourage further analysis of our calling.

## REFERENCES

Bagley, A. (Ed.). (1975). *The professor of education: An assessment of conditions*. Minneapolis: Society of Professors of Education, College of Education, University of Minnesota.

Carnegie Forum (1986). *A nation prepared: Teachers for the twenty-first Century* (Report of the Task Force on Teaching as a Profession). New York: Carnegie Corporation.

Clark, B. R. (1987). *The academic life: Small worlds, different worlds*. Princeton, N.J.: The Carnegie Foundation for the Advancement of Teaching.

Holmes Group (1985). *Tomorrow's teachers: A report of the Holmes Group*. East Lansing, Mich.: The Holmes Group.

Judge, H.(1982). *American graduate schools of education: A view from abroad*. New York: The Ford Foundation.

Ladd, E. C., Jr., & Lipset, S. M. (1975). *The divided academy: Professors and politics* [Carnegie Commission on Higher Education]. New York: McGraw-Hill Book Company.

Lortie, D. (1975). *Schoolteacher: A Sociological Study.* Chicago: University of Chicago Press.

Magrath, C., & Egbert, R. (Eds.). (1987). *Strengthening teacher education: The challenges to college and university leaders.* San Francisco: Jossey-Bass Publishers.

Morgan, G. (Ed.). (1983). *Beyond method: Strategies for social research.* Beverly Hills, Calif.: Sage Publications.

Powell, A. G. (1980). *The uncertain profession: Harvard and the search for educational authority.* Cambridge, Mass.: Harvard University Press.

Raths, J. D., & Katz, L. G. (Eds.). (1985). *Advances in teacher education* (Vol. 2). Norwood, N.J.: Ablex Publishing Corp.

Ryan, K. (Ed.). (1975). *Teacher education* (74th Yearbook of the National Society for the Study of Education). Chicago: University of Chicago Press.

# 2

# Education Professors: The Centennial of an Identity Crisis

## J. STEPHEN HAZLETT

The education professoriate is about 100 years old. In 1879, the University of Michigan established a chair in the science and art of teaching. Its first incumbent, William H. Payne, is sometimes credited with having been the first professor of education. There had been earlier collegiate positions in education, but they failed to take root. Some were in normal or preparatory departments and thus not considered to be truly part of the university, or they were appendages to appointments in other fields such as philosophy or psychology. These early efforts produced either transitory results or failed to secure an independent status for education in the university.

Following the University of Michigan's action, other institutions took similar steps, and by 1890 there were 31 professors of education in the country. During the 1890s, the number increased, and at the turn of the century it was possible to pursue a doctorate in the subject at a few universities (Johanningmeier & Johnson, 1975). The year 1890 is a convenient date for the establishment of the American education professoriate. By then, there were enough education professors for the field to have a foothold in the academy, and the possibility was entertained, albeit grudgingly in many quarters, that education might develop into a respectable university study.

If 1890 is accepted as a founding date, a centennial is at hand. It is an appropriate time for taking stock, for reviewing the growth and accomplishments of the field, for reflecting upon the status and characteristics of the professional community, and for laying plans to guide its future.

A complete accounting of the education professoriate cannot be given. This is so, in part, because the requisite information base is still fragmentary. There is no comprehensive study of the origins and development of the education professoriate. The available historical sketches, institutional histories, and scattered references which touch upon the subject are useful and suggestive but insufficient to permit a general understanding of the professoriate's past (Cronbach, 1969; Johnson & Johanningmeier, 1972; Lynch, 1946; Powell, 1980; Sizer & Powell, 1969). Moreover, frameworks for interpreting the movements of the field and the activities of its laborers remain to be elaborated. The historiography of the education professoriate is still in a formative stage. Before historical assertions about the generality of the professional grouping can be confidently made, more bibliographic and archival sources will have to be examined and a stronger foundation of studies laid.

Similar comments apply to the statements about education professors contained in the nonhistorical literature. Bibliographic searches yield a strange catch of disparate items: books and papers dealing with university professors in general, faculty careers and development, teacher education, educational research, professionalization, educational reform, faculty productivity and time use, and schools of education. For the most part, education professors are shadowy figures tied to an important undertaking but not outstanding in their own right.

In the majority of these works, education professors are lost in the larger confraternity, mentioned only in passing, treated obliquely in reference to other concerns (e.g., research or teacher education), or are present mainly by implication or extension. Only a small minority bears directly and primarily on the education professoriate. These studies have been episodic, not consciously building on each other, and varied as to starting points, methodologies, and findings.

Consequently, detailing a clear picture of education professors is not possible at present. To do so would require a corpus of related, sequential, and mutually informed studies, and this has not been developed over the past century. The purposes here, in consequence, are only to note prominent statements made about the education professoriate and to offer speculations regarding them.

Writings on the professoriate tend to fall into three genres: those that focus on the characteristics of the professoriate, those that seek to define the role, and those that deal with a range of conceptual and/or descriptive matters.

## STUDIES OF PROFESSORIAL CHARACTERISTICS

Counelis's (1969) "The Professoriate in the Discipline of Education" is an instance of the first genre. Drawing heavily on surveys and statistical reports, Counelis sought information about education professors as professionals, their deployment in higher education, and their work. He found them to be older, less intellectually apt, but more broadly educated at the undergraduate level than their colleagues elsewhere in the university. Their primary activity was teacher education, and their efforts were judged a qualified success quantitatively and qualitatively. With regard to graduate education and research, however, Counelis observed that fewer education professors possessed the doctorate than their counterparts in other fields, that doctoral programs in education produced few researchers, and therefore that the research output of education professors was "less than optimal."

In 1975, another characteristics study focused on social background and career pattern differences between male and female professors of education. (Weidman & Weidman, 1975). Among the variables considered were social class, marital status, possession of the doctorate, rank, salary, and scholarly productivity. Consistent discrimination against women in terms of rank and salary was a noteworthy finding of this study.

A more recent example in this line of investigation is the work of Ducharme and Agne, discussed later in this volume. On the basis of questionnaire data, they reported on the preparation, experience, work load, scholarly productivity, and "place in higher education" of 340 respondents (Ducharme & Agne, 1982). Contrary to the conclusions of earlier studies, these authors found the education professors they surveyed to be largely qualified with the doctorate and generally as prolific in publication as their colleagues in other fields. Moreover, they contradicted the assumption that education professors lack public school experience with the finding that 71 percent of their respondents had held full-time positions in the schools before launching their college or university careers. Subsequent to their 1982 study, these authors have continued their research with inquiry into social class background, sex differences, teaching load, and other factors.

Adams and Hord collected data in 1984 on education professors in three types of institutions (state colleges, land-grant universities, and private institutions) with regard to faculty characteristics, work load, service, and professional activities (Adams & Hord, 1985). They reported that professors in private institutions have more school experience and less higher education experience than their colleagues elsewhere; that more than 90 percent of all teacher education professors have no research assignment as part of their work loads; that professors in land-grant institutions produce the most publications and have the most on-going research, yet state college professors more frequently make presentations at professional meetings; and that about one-third of all teacher education professors supervise student teachers. They offered no interpretation of these and other findings.

As part of a study of research on teacher education, Lanier (1984) discussed characteristics of education professors and attempted to advance an interpretation of them. She noted the low esteem in which most education professors are held, their perennial quarrels with their colleagues in other departments, and the excessively practical orientation, bordering on anti-intellectualism, with which they approach their work. These observations have, of course, been made many times before. But Lanier went further (as Ducharme and Agne have subsequently done) and linked these characteristics to the lower-middle-class background of most professors of education. This background, it was argued, tends to produce a cultural and psychological bias favoring conservatism, a conformist orientation, and a utilitarian view of knowledge. Previous experience working in rule-governed bureaucratized schools reinforces this bias education professors then perpetuate among their students, who come in large measure from the same social class background. This mentality, derived from the interpenetration of social class, home climate, child-rearing practices, life in schools, and traditional role expectations for females, helps to account, in Lanier's opinion, for some of the salient traits of education professors as well as for why these professors do not always feel comfortable in the university, where theory, abstraction, and inquiry are prized. Although Lanier did not press her case (it was only one aspect of the subject she was addressing), it is provocative. It represents an effort, not usually found in studies of this type, to provide a conceptual framework for dealing with observations and data.

The above are examples of the characteristics literature. Others may be found in this volume, and the pace of their appearance seems to be increasing as more scholars turn their attention to the nature of the education professoriate. Studies in this vein are unquestionably useful and worthy of pursuit. Additional knowledge of the education professors' backgrounds, their activities, and how they see themselves is needed so that a clearer, more detailed profile of the group might emerge.

## PROBLEMS OF DEFINITION

Two serious problems hobble this line of investigation. The first is the frail sense of identity existing among those referred to as education professors. Despite a century of survival, the education professoriate lacks adequate definition and delimitation. There is no satisfactory answer to the question, who is a professor of education? Is it the professor who teaches methods courses? If so, what of faculty members in arts and sciences who perform this task—are they education professors? What about the historians, mathematicians, geographers, and English scholars who regularly deal with students, sometimes in special classes, preparing to teach these subjects? And psychologists, whether in education schools or across campus, who give instruction in child development, learning theory, or the more global educational psychology? And professors, wherever housed, who teach statistics, educational history, the philosophy of education, and other so-called foundational studies? And curriculum theorists, professors of school administration, media specialists, and professors of counseling? And what about the supervisors of student teachers? They sometimes hold professorial rank, sometimes they do not, and some are classroom teachers working in association with the university.

Can all or just some of the persons playing these roles be legitimately subsumed under the title "education professor"? If the former, then the problem of identity remains, for it is obvious that the orientations, values, standards of work, and professional associations of these groupings are dissimilar; the cleavages within the professoriate, so defined, are as sharp as those separating it from other professorial communities. If the latter is the correct approach, then three questions immediately come to the fore: Where does one draw the line in setting the roles apart? On what basis is the line drawn? And why, in the past century, has not this distinction been achieved?

The second problem is related to the first. Lacking a shared understanding of who education professors are, it is difficult to assess properly what they are supposed to do. Therefore, cataloguing their characteristics, although necessary and interesting, is limited and of uncertain significance. The reader of several characteristics studies may well conclude, "So what?" What does it matter that education professors enter their careers older than other professors, or that they have considerable public school experience, or that they spend long hours in their offices, or that they did not publish much in the past but are doing more now? Each of these traits is subject to widely varying evaluations as to appropriateness or inappropriateness. A relatively slight publication record may lead to lower university esteem, but it may also indicate that the professor has more time to work with students in clinical settings and to offer needed inservice education for teachers. A lower-middle-class background may influence one's academic aspirations (although it is hard to accept that it *ipso facto* renders one intellectually less able), but it may enhance one's sensitivity to the teaching and learning problems encountered in mass education. It may even increase one's effectiveness in working with schools.

The point is that without broadly shared expectations and standards concerning what education professors are supposed to be about in their professional activity, a list of their characteristics does not get us very far. Until it is decided who is truly an education professor, these expectations and standards will continue to be elusive.

Lanier and Ducharme and Agne are among the authors aware of the constitutional difficulties. Lanier (1984) began her study in search of the true education professor. Ducharme and Agne (1982) referred to the great variation in roles, interests, and occupational settings among the members of the professoriate and commented on an "unsettled feeling" about education professors resulting in "conflicting descriptions and expectations about what they do, what their preparation and background are, and what measures of quality may be appropriate."

## CONCEPTUAL STUDIES

These problems lead directly to the third category of writings about the education professoriate. This type is analytical, conceptual, and prescriptive. One of the early entries is a piece by James Earl Russell reflecting in 1924 on his twenty-seven year tenure as dean of Teachers College, Columbia University (Borrowman, 1975). Russell analyzed the tension in his institution between professors of "academic" and "professional" orientations. The former prized systematic knowledge, its cultivation and expansion, while the latter dwelt on training and valued knowledge, from whatever source, in terms of its utility on the job. The differences in perspective manifested themselves in many ways, and the administrator presiding over the two camps was lucky if he could "get on without bloodshed." Russell's solution was for the problem to go away, for each side to understand and to appreciate the other. He opined that when the two came to call each other friends the millennium would have almost arrived. Russell's essay set the stage for subsequent contributions. The analysis of divisions within the education professoriate followed by proposals for lessening tension and for better organizing the profession became a model for this branch of the literature.

Forty-five years after Russell, Sizer and Powell wrote similarly about "field-oriented" and "disciplinary" professors and commented on the persistent friction between the two (Sizer & Powell, 1969). They did not argue for an end to specialization. Instead, they called for a fusion within individuals of differing styles of thought and inquiry so that the gap between practice and academics might be bridged for the mutual benefit of practitioners and the professoriate.

The configuration of the education professoriate and the divisions therein continue to be the objects of reflection and analysis (Borrowman, 1975; Jackson, 1975: Judge, 1982; Reagan, 1975; Roemer & Martinello, 1982). In addition to pleas for making peace, fusion, bridging gaps, and transcending differences, new conceptions for organizing education faculties have also been proposed. Seeing education professors standing between the university and the schools, Borrowman (1975) suggested the distinction between critic and actor. For him, school personnel are the doers, the actors on stage; professors are critics, those who explain, evaluate, and offer advice. The role of the school of education is "to mediate the critical and operational functions." Jackson (1975) offered a tripartite schema of the professoriate composed of "disciplinists," "generalists" (whose expertise may be drawn from several subjects and whose focus is on a category of schooling or education, e.g., educational administration, curriculum, or higher education), and "pedagogists" (who are concerned with the techniques and materials involved in the teaching of various subjects, e.g., science teaching, music education, etc.). Differences are found among and within these groups, and a major source of difficulty stems from the misguided effort to arrange the groups hierarchically. Such efforts merely energize the old game of who is the most important, instead of recognizing the value of each to the profession.

Jackson hedged on proposing a solution and doubted the efficacy of the notion put forth by Sizer and Powell that things would get better if the members of each group would learn more of the other's world. Besides questioning the likelihood of this ever happening, he was skeptical of what would be accomplished even if such "fusion" were to take place: would a stint in an elementary classroom make an educational historian a better historian? In his opinion, the most pressing concern lay elsewhere—with the intellectual quality of the education professor's work in whatever camp he or she might be in. It was not a question, for Jackson, of theory or practice or fostering a greater appreciation of the two. It was a matter of "old-fashioned virtues having to do with clarity of thought and expression in both." The well-being of the education professoriate ultimately depended on manifesting its intelligence, broadly considered as the "expression of orderly and tough-minded inquiry."

Thus, this ill-defined profession limps along. Occasionally, someone points to the problem, subjects it to scrutiny, suggests a remedy or steps toward a remedy, and issues a plea for the professoriate to get its collective act together, followed by a warning that failure to do so will lead to dire consequences.

Interestingly, the conceptual and reformist literature has had little noticeable impact. For one thing, the papers and articles in this genre have been "nondevelopmental"; there has been much independent ploughing and reploughing of the same ground. A more telling observation is that the works have failed to ignite a collective effort on the part of education professors more clearly to define, delimit, and organize themselves. The situation described by Russell in 1924 (Borrowman, 1975), by Sizer and Powell (1969), and by Jackson (1975) is materially the same as that of the present. Their words have a timeless quality.

Explaining a sense of *ennui* regarding these matters is not likely to be successful without a closer examination of the nature of professional education as a field and of the circumstances of its entry into higher education. Where early professorships in education were established in the late nineteenth century, it was hoped and expected that these professors would develop a discipline of education. The expectation was realistic. At that time, a number of disciplines, particularly in the social sciences, were emerging and beginning to assume distinctive identities. The idea of creating a special body of theory and knowledge peculiar to education seemed reasonable. Early scholars in the field, such as Payne and Dewey, set about the task, outlined research, and proposed connections with other fields from which relevant theoretical considerations and knowledge could be appropriated for the fledgling study.

Some of the early workers looked to history and philosophy to anchor their undertaking, while others championed the cause of a more scientific body of knowledge based on careful observation and experimentation. It was a time of promise, for even those who doubted the viability of a true "science" of education, such as Josiah Royce and Charles Eliot, did not deny that it was possible to study, to teach, and to learn something about education.

Formulating a field of scholarship was not the only reason for accepting education in the university. More immediate and practical concerns were also at stake. One was the need to prepare additional teachers for the rapidly growing and expanding secondary schools. Although normal schools might assume this responsibility, there were strong arguments against this solution and in favor of vesting the task with the university. Rhodes and Eisele (1986) summarized these arguments. Institutions of higher education offered the best conditions for study and scholarship, for producing educators of broad culture and learning and capable of providing leadership, for professionalizing the occupation of teaching, for recruiting the most desirable candidates, and for furthering the professional preparation of those who were already in place as teachers. Training, educational reform, professionalization, and the advancement of scholarship were thus intermingled in this campaign.

## HARVARD'S PAUL HENRY HANUS

Powell's (1980) history of professional education at Harvard illuminates these motives and the conundrums their interaction posed. This discussion relies heavily on his work. In the late nineteenth century, President Eliot was concerned about the quality of the students applying for admission to Harvard. He wanted better prepared students for the increasingly specialized and advanced curricula of the university, and he also sought to free faculty members from having to teach elementary courses in their specialties. Following the principle that the schools should follow the university, Eliot and members of the faculty engaged in a number of what today would be called school improvement projects. They also accepted the challenge of having Harvard do more in the way of teacher training, believing that better prepared teachers would surely produce better prepared students. Their motivation, therefore, had nothing to do with a discipline of education. Rather, it stemmed from the practical desire to do what would be good for Harvard.

During the 1890–91 academic year, Harvard established a "normal course" and then hired Paul Henry Hanus to coordinate its teacher education program (Powell, 1980). Hanus, who had studied science and mathematics at the University of Michigan and had been a professor of mathematics and pedagogy, had also been a druggist and the principal of a Denver high school. He was brought to Harvard not for his scholarly potential but as an administrative convenience, as someone to take charge of the details of teacher education. Not surprisingly, he had some difficulty deciding what to teach and was forced, in his own words, quoted by Powell, to "spin largely from my own substance" (p. 54). This was not an easy task, as he soon discovered. Instruction in curriculum, methods, and psychology was ensconced in academic departments. When he trod too close to these domains, he got into trouble and, on occasion, was attacked by his colleagues for undermining their work and for the pretentiousness of some of his pedagogical claims ("The chief trouble," Barrett Wendell once complained, was "old-fashioned ignorance, not neglect of 'pedagogy' " [p. 62].)

In an environment little supportive of fostering the growth of education as a discipline (a project in which he seems to have had only limited interest himself), Hanus turned to discoursing on the aims of education. He devoted more of his energy to coordination, promotional activities, and the cause of school reform. His courses attracted few students, and he had to live with the realization that the university was routinely turning out teachers who had never set foot in his classroom.

By the turn of the century, Hanus had shifted his ground and was arguing that Harvard should train school administrators. This agenda was appealing in several respects. As city school systems grew in size and complexity in a society that seemed to be changing in bewildering ways, the need for more administrators and educational leaders was readily apparent. Focusing on the preparation of higher-echelon educators also appeared to be a more expeditious approach to promoting school reform. Moreover, there was the fact— one not to be ignored—that the training of administrators held little interest for the arts and sciences faculty and was thus a territory in which education professors could safely take their stand.

In a twenty-year period at Harvard, Hanus moved from being a coordinator and teacher educator to being a specialist in school administration. By 1910, he considered himself an expert in the school superintendency. In the process, he shifted his intellectual orientation as well. He started and then abandoned research projects in the history and philosophy of education; he then failed to pick up on opportunities to do work in psychology. By the time he was claiming expertise in educational administration, he was looking outside the university to the problems of the schools and to the demands of the careers therein for the sources of his professorial inspiration.

This brief synopsis of the early years of the education professoriate at Harvard, drawn from Powell's intriguing study, cannot be generalized with confidence. Too much is unknown to posit firm parallels, and all universities did not evolve in the same manner or share the same climate. In institutions derived from normal schools, for example, the press for scholarship does not seem to have been particularly great (at least not until recent years), and education professors there have played a larger and more respected role in the conduct of university affairs. Indeed, in some institutions at least, in the progression from normal school through state teachers college and state college to state university, the normal school survived as a foundation. Scratch the surface of the university and the old habits, standards, and ways of doing things shine through.

The Harvard experience is not unique. Education professors in other institutions wrestled in similar fashion with many of the same problems Hanus faced, as discussed in the next chapter by Allison. This historical episode places the questions surrounding the identity of education professors in an interesting perspective and prompts a provocative agenda for research.

At the risk of exaggeration, it may be suggested that Harvard accepted a professor of education but not his field. Eliot hired Hanus, protected him, secured his reappointment, and encouraged him. Although he believed that there was something to teach in education, Eliot maintained his skepticism about the field as an independent discipline, and Harvard did little to foster its cultivation as such. Hanus may be faulted for lack of assiduous effort on the task, but the point should not be overdrawn. The conditions in which he worked were plainly unfavorable, and no one individual can create a field single-handedly. If Payne and Dewey were equally unsuccessful, blaming Hanus for his failure must be tempered. Knowing more about the circumstances under which professors of education came into the university is necessary in order to understand the current status of the field and its incumbents.

If the situation at Harvard proves to be representative, the problem of defining a professor of education may have had a constitutional flaw from the start. Hanus did not confront a *tabula rasa* awaiting his imprint. Many of his colleagues were in the business of teacher education and were unwilling to defer to any presumed expertise of the new arrival. The familiar posture to the effect that teacher education is an all-university affair was in place from the very beginning. Therefore, Hanus had to accommodate the status quo and to carve out a niche for himself on unoccupied ground. The extent of accommodation, of taking a stand in areas which others do not want, is another topic deserving a closer look.

## CRITICISMS OF EDUCATION

Resistance to professional education involved more than defending territory, however. It involved even more than the natural skepticism of the potential of a new field or of the hopes for a science of education. In joining the ranks of the university faculty, education professors ran into the long-standing and deeply rooted cultural bias against the needfulness of pedagogical training. This was *not* a manifestation of American anti-intellectualism, for the bias was shared by professors, who certainly valued scholarship, inquiry, and the life of the mind. Rather it was the belief that effective teaching did not entail more than a command of subject matter, common sense, and a measure of empathy with one's students.

The notion that good teaching required study and professional training was a threat. First, it was a threat to professors who earned their living as teachers without the benefit of formal pedagogical preparation. Beyond that, it was and is a threat to the American faith in education to solve societal and personal problems. Americans have long tended to see their problems in educational terms and to assume that educating people to do the right thing offers the most effective solutions. To be sure, schools have a large responsibility, but so do parents, public officials, civic and religious leaders, the media, and advocacy organizations. To interpose the idea that good teaching must be informed by specialized, disciplinary study risks diminishing the faith in a strategy on which so much seems to depend. Perhaps this is why, despite evidence in its behalf, the idea has been ignored, contemptuously rejected, or treated derisively.

One hundred years of work by education professors has not altered this bias. In all the current talk about improving schools and teaching, there are those who would lengthen teacher preparation and make it more rigorous. There are others, equally sincere, who believe that one step toward reform is to circumvent or dismantle conventional teacher education, asserting that pedagogical courses are vapid and unnecessary obstacles keeping talented persons from becoming teachers. Without the hindrance of such courses, talented people will more easily come to teaching, and education will be improved. Hence plans for "alternative certification" and proposals for reforming teacher education out of existence. Journalists, politicians, and even university officials and educational leaders express this bias. A United States secretary of education described subject matter competence, the ability to communicate, and sound character as "the three fundamental, irreducible requirements for teaching in our schools" and then urged that the job be opened up to capable persons who "do not possess this paper credential or that" (Bennett, 1986, p. 6).

## DEVELOPMENT OF THE PROFESSORIATE

The early attempts to construct a discipline of education were short-lived. By the third decade of the twentieth century, education professors had turned, as had Hanus, from the quest for a discipline to what has been termed the occupational standard (Katz, 1966). They became preoccupied with training for and serving occupational roles in the rapidly expanding bureaucracy of the public schools. Their specialties in the university came to mirror these occupational roles; hence, professors of elementary education, secondary education, guidance and counseling, pupil personnel services, and elementary school administration. A narrowing and a broadening occurred simultaneously. As professors focussed on specific roles in the schools, their proclaimed expertise expanded so that they might prepare practitioners for each role. The practical needs of the occupation became the standard for what was taught in schools of education.

Under these conditions, the search for a discipline atrophied. Those most likely to pursue this goal were swept together in "foundations" groupings and were uneasily attached to the occupational orientation of their more numerous colleagues. As the specializations were increasingly refined, communication and understanding among professors became more difficult, and tension grew between professors of differing occupational specialties. But did this have to happen? Notwithstanding constraints and prejudice, to what extent did education professors choose, as opposed to being pushed, to neglect theorizing about education and to embrace the occupational standard and become adjuncts of the schools?

Another line of inquiry is perhaps more engaging. Despite its constitutional and organizational defects, the stresses within it, the persistent criticisms of it coming from all sides, and its precarious status within the university, the education professoriate has survived. How can this be so? How can the continued existence of a profession that supposedly suffers fatal flaws be explained?

If the narrative of the professoriate's evolution is shadowy, this topic is more obscure. The present literature offers only hints and, as might be expected, none of them has to do with intellection and scholarship. The key to the education professoriate's survival may pertain more to its functions than to its purposes. Recall that Hanus was brought to Harvard as an "administrative convenience" to coordinate activities whose ultimate aim was to increase the supply of qualified students for the university.

Borrowman (1975) has suggested that the education professoriate is the result of demographic pressure. It arose at a time when there was an unusually large demand for school personnel and was tolerated because it supplied this quantitative need. Now that the pressure has eased, however, the professoriate's reason for being may have been lost. Arts and science professors can teach the theoretics of education, and practitioners in the schools—many of whom possess credentials and expertise equal to those of education professors—can adequately handle the practical aspects of training.

Another tack suggests the legitimizing function of the education professoriate. According to Sizer and Powell (1969), after 1890, the new schools of education sought recruits for the professoriate from the swelling ranks of teachers and administrators. Once inducted, these professors strove to secure and defend the public school and helped legitimize it and themselves in a symbiotic relationship by making a university credential one of the qualifications for holding various positions in the lower schools. Two sustaining forces are at work here: the symbolic value of affiliation with the university and its prestige, and the power which flows from control over credentialing. From this point of view, the quality of what is taught and what is learned in a school of education is not critical. What really explains keeping education professors in work and students in class are the degree and the credential.

Yet, another approach sees the rise of the education professoriate as part of the democratization of higher education. Normal schools, it has been argued, did not just train teachers; they provided opportunities for advanced education to those not likely to attend college (Herbst, 1980). Extending this argument, perhaps the same thing happened after professional education moved into the university. Schools of education welcomed uncertain, marginal students and led them toward a university degree by training them for an occupation many of them would never enter. In this manner the education professoriate has been maintained, and the presumed softness of its field has enhanced its functional utility.

If nonacademic functions have sustained the education professoriate, their diminution would be perilous. Borrowman's and other analyses cannot be ignored: education professors could be in decline. On the other hand, another future may be possible. Notwithstanding prejudice to the contrary, one can plausibly contend that the study of education, including pedagogy, is a worthwhile intellectual pursuit. Much evidence indicates that it is. While not adequately developed, the study of education is indeed productive of knowledge and insights contributory to informed, thoughtful educational practice.

## CONCLUSION

For a better future to be possible, education professors must take the initiative. Mumbling and grumbling, handwringing, noble rhetoric, and a desire to be helpful in any way will not suffice. Berliner's (1984) critique of teacher educators is apt. He accuses them of lacking passion, lacking vision, and, most of all, of timidity. They are timid in dealing with research, in exercising professional judgment in the face of clearly inferior educational practices. That they do not actively pursue new knowledge is too bad; that they do not act responsibly on the knowledge they already possess is a devastating indictment. Taking the initiative calls first and foremost for courage.

A second step is overdue and inescapable. The field of education must be defined and delimited. There is no great mystery about the way this is done. Intellectual historians have traced the stages in the case of several professions (Bledstein, 1976; Haskell, 1977). Associates in a common enterprise argue and debate, propose and dispose, organize and disorganize, until eventually the outlines of the field are clear. These outlines are not discovered; they are manufactured, intellectually and politically. The associates of the growing community thus define the field and are thereby defined themselves by it. Not everyone can be a member. As the field develops its unique lore and intellectual substance, competence therein determines membership in the professional community, distinguishing the professional from the amateur. The field sets the boundaries for the work of its adherents; embodies what is considered to be truthful, valuable, and relevant knowledge; sets the questions for inquiry as well as the approaches for pursuing them; and posits standards of credibility and quality. In this way, a distinct professional community and professional culture evolve.

To repeat, the field is created by its members and, in turn, regulates their professional identity and behavior. This has not happened within the education professoriate. A distinctive professional lore and culture have not been created to help it become a distinctive professional community. The result has been the oft-noted and oft-lamented lack of definition of the group. Although unfortunate this is not surprising. A poorly defined professoriate is a logical consequence of a poorly defined field. To understand education professors and the expectations and standards to which they should aspire, the field must be better formulated.

My conclusions are unfortunately stale. They include a call for more research and yet another plea for education professors to attend to their calling. By learning more about their origins and work, professors can shape the community of scholars. There can, of course, be no assurance of success. Perhaps it is too late. Perhaps the task is too difficult. But it is worth a try, as exemplified by Allison's study in the next chapter. It is to be hoped that at the end of the next one hundred years, education professors will have a proud history, not just a past.

## REFERENCES

Adams, R., & Hord, S. (1985, October). *A workshop on the professoriate.* Paper presented at the annual meeting of the Teacher Education Council of State Colleges and Universities, St. Louis, Mo.

Bennett spells out basic criteria for teachers. (1986). *Teacher Education Reports, 8* (6), 6–7.

Berliner, D. C. (1984, October). *Contemporary teacher education: Timidity, lack of vision and ignorance.* Paper presented at the meeting of the National Academy of Education. Berkeley, Calif.

Bledstein, B. J. (1976). *The culture of professionalism: The middle class and the development of higher education in America.* New York: W. W. Norton & Co.

Borrowman, M. L. (1975). About professors of education. In A. Bagley (Ed.), *The professor of education: An assessment of conditions* (pp. 55–60). Minneapolis: Society of Professors of Education, College of Education, University of Minnesota.

Counelis, J. S. (1969). The professoriate in the discipline of education. In J. S. Counelis (Ed.), *To be a Phoenix: The education professoriate* (pp. 1–29). Bloomington, Ind.: Phi Delta Kappa.

Cronbach, L. J., & Suppes, P. (Eds.). (1969). *Research for tomorrow's schools: Disciplined inquiry for education.* New York: Macmillan Company.

Ducharme, E. R., & Agne, R. M. (1982). The education professoriate: A research based perspective. *Journal of Teacher Education, 33* (November–December), 30–36.

Haskell, T. L. (1977). *The emergence of professional social science: The American Social Science Association and nineteenth-century crisis of authority.* Urbana: University of Illinois Press.

Jackson, P. W. (1975). Divided we stand: Observations on the internal organization of the education professoriate. In A. Bagley (Ed.), *The professor of education: An assessment of conditions* (pp. 61–70). Minneapolis: Society of Professors of Education, College of Education, University of Minnesota.

Johanningmeier, E. V., & Johnson, H. C., Jr. (1975). The education professoriate: A historical consideration of its work and growth. In A. Bagley (Ed.), *The professor of education: an assessment of conditions* (pp. 2–18). Minneapolis: Society of Professors of Education, College of Education, University of Minnesota.

Johnson, H. C., Jr., & Johanningmeier, E. V. (1972). *Teachers for the prairie: The University of Illinois and the schools, 1868–1945.* Urbana: University of Illinois Press.

Judge, H. (1982). *American graduate schools of education: A view from abroad.* New York: The Ford Foundation.

Katz, M. B. (1966). From theory to survey in graduate schools of education. *Journal of Higher Education, 36,* 325–334.

Lanier, J. E. (1984). *Research on teacher education* (Occasional Paper No. 80). East Lansing, Mich.: Institute for Research on Teaching, Michigan State University.

Lynch, W. O. (1946). *A history of Indiana State Teachers College, 1865–1945.* Terre Haute: Indiana State Teachers College.

Powell, A. G. (1980). *The uncertain profession: Harvard and the search for educational authority.* Cambridge, Mass.: Harvard University Press.

Reagan, J. M. (1975). Education professoriate: The concept, some problems and some proposals. In A. Bagley (Ed.), *The Professor of Education: An assessment of conditions* (pp. 29–52). Minneapolis: Society of Professors of Education, College of Education, University of Minnesota.

Rhodes, D., & Eisele, C. (1986, February). *Preparing teachers for the twentieth century: Lessons from an unmet challenge of the past.* A paper presented at the annual meeting of the Association of Teacher Educators, Atlanta, Ga.

Roemer, R. E., & Martinello, M. L. (1982). Divisions in the educational professoriate and the future of professional education. *Educational Studies, 13* (Summer), 203–23.

Sizer, T. R., & Powell, A. G. (1969). Changing conceptions of the professor of education. In J. S. Counelis (Ed.), *To be a Phoenix: The education professoriate* (pp. 61-76). Bloomington, Ind.: Phi Delta Kappa.

Weidman, C. S., & Weidman, J. C. (1975). Professors of education: Some social and occupational characteristics. In A. Bagley (Ed.), *The professor of education: An assessment of conditions* (pp. 87–101). Minneapolis: Society of Professors of Education, College of Education, University of Minnesota.

# 3

# Early Professors of Education: Three Case Studies

## CLINTON B. ALLISON

### INTRODUCTION

In the previous chapter, Hazlett argues that neither general under-
standings nor interpretative frameworks have been sufficiently developed to support a history of the educational professoriate. To have
such a history, we need biographies of education professors. Commenting on historiography in education, Greene (1973) writes of the
need for both contours and identities, for generalizations and interpretations that explain the particular, and for close examination of
individual persons who acted or were acted upon.

The contours on the education professoriate are not clearly defined. Sufficient reliable information is lacking to generalize with confidence about several fundamental questions. How were early teacher
educators alike or different from other professors? What of their

scholarship? Their sense of mission? Their relationship with the university community?

We need identities around which to build our history, the stories of particular professors at different institutions and times. To direct some light on Hazlett's "shadowy figure" of the education professor, the biographies of three professors at the University of Tennessee are offered in this chapter: Thomas C. Karns (1886–1899), Philander P. Claxton (1902–1911), and Benjamin O. Duggan (1922–1939). These biographies are illustrations of the historical sketches needed before a full understanding of the educational professoriate emerges.

These professors are not treated as samples of a social type for purposes of testing generalizations found in the literature. Wolff (1979) warns that such attempts are presumptuous, that we cannot fit a person "smoothly to the shape of other characters of his 'type' . . . like a geared key into the lock of received expectations." Even so, they exhibited in their professional lives many of the salient characteristics of the education professoriate as described elsewhere. These professors were more parochial than most of their colleagues in other disciplines. They were all born and reared on Tennessee farms. They received their undergraduate degrees from the state university where they later taught. Only one earned a master's degree, none held a doctorate.

They made their significant contributions in professional service rather than in scholarship. None made an original contribution to scholarship. Indeed, they engaged in little intellectual inquiry. They were more esteemed outside the university, particularly among school teachers and administrators, than with their campus colleagues in other departments.

Like professors of education of their generation elsewhere, Karns and Claxton helped to create pedagogy as an academic field of study. All three were forced to defend teacher education from a suspicious liberal arts faculty and an often unfriendly university administration.

## THOMAS CONNER KARNS:
### NINETEENTH-CENTURY PROFESSOR OF PEDAGOGY

Thomas C. Karns was the professor of pedagogy at the University of Tennessee in the 1890s. A prominent faculty member, he often performed the duties of the frequently absent president, Charles W.

Dabney. One of Eastern Tennessee's best known "scholars," the genial Karns was a popular speaker at teachers' meetings, farmers' conventions, and other rural meetings.

Because they were often invited to the university after successful public school experience, nineteenth-century professors of pedagogy were often local residents. Karns grew up on a farm fewer than ten miles from the University of Tennessee. Typhoid fever in adolescence, exacerbated by an infection (known then as white swellings), left him lame and often in pain throughout life. Karns was salutatorian in the first graduating class of the University after the Civil War, an honor mitigated by the fact that there were only four graduates that year, all in the classical curriculum.

As was common in the nineteenth century, Karns pursued several occupations. He was a journalist before and after his tenure as a school administrator and professor. Following college, he was a reporter (and sometimes editorial writer) on newspapers in Knoxville, Chattanooga, and Nashville. In his later years, he was agricultural editor of the *Knoxville Journal and Tribune*, writing a farm column under the pen name Uncle Zeke. A rural life enthusiast, he was always a part-time farmer. "Karns off in the country somewhere," Dabney (1896) grumbled to a correspondent.

His career as an educator was also varied. He taught many unrelated disciplines and moved back and forth from administration to teaching and from lower to college levels. In 1873, the Tennessee Public School System was created, replacing school districts with a county system. Karns, at age twenty-eight, was elected Knox County Superintendent of Public Schools. From 1875 to 1877, he taught in the preparatory department of The University of Tennessee, and from 1877 to 1881 at the Masonic Institute (a normal school) at Cleveland, Tennessee. He later served as a principal and superintendent of schools in eastern Tennessee. An earnest Baptist, he was professor of English and modern languages at a local Baptist college, Carson and Newman, before returning to the University of Tennessee in 1886 as principal of the preparatory department. He was elected principal of the new teachers' department in 1893 and remained at the University until his resignation in 1899.

He was the most popular professor in the Summer Normal Institutes held under the auspices of the University in the 1880s and 1890s. Karns appears to have done the best job of balancing subject content and teaching methodology. His "talks" on algebra, geography, and history were, according to the local newspaper, "practical and to the point"; his lessons on teaching children by the word and script method were extremely popular with teachers, especially when he used a real "class of little ones" to demonstrate his methods (Allison, 1983b).

Because he was lame, Karns, who never married, was given a room in an academic building, South College, to use as a study-bedroom. Later he moved off campus (Parham-McCoy, 1929):

> As his crippled limb kept him from walking to the University he acquired a horse and buggy, also a young colored by [sic] to look after horse and his owner. This horse, a beautiful, spirited by [bay] and Hurt, the darkey [sic], became almost as well known as Professor Karns himself. Hurt drove his master up to the University buildings in the mornings, came for him at noon, took him back, then called for him again in the afternoon. He also kept the horse and buggy well groomed and took care of his employer's rooms and person.

An enigma in Karns's professorship was his silence on a most controversial issue of the early 1890s, the admission of women to the University. At first, women were admitted only to the teachers' department; yet, he seems to have nothing to say, at least publicly, on the debate.

In his first year as principal, Karns (1893b) assured Dabney that after an examination of education departments throughout the country, he was developing "an ideal course which shall embrace the entire science and art of pedagogy." To demonstrate that pedagogy was a science, he conducted experiments "from the scientific point of view" in educational psychology; unfortunately the nature of these experiments is unknown (Of Local Interest, 1894). As part of his devotion to science, Karns (1893b) accepted Social Darwinism as a "proposition . . . so evident as to demand no further argument." He explained to Dabney that every school "must be adopted to its environment, . . . this principle holds in the evolution of culture as well as in the evolution of animal life." His aim for the teacher education curriculum was a "strict harmony with both scientific theory and practical results."

Initial support for the department by Dabney and the enthusiastic commitment to his new duties as principal by Karns were demonstrated by the creation of a pedagogical museum. During the summer of 1894, quarters for Karns's department were refurbished. He was given the entire lower floor of Old College, consisting of a "beautiful new lecture-room," and reading room and a library/museum—all "handsomely fitted up" (Of Local Interest, 1894).

Karns (1894) wished to have a first-rate educational library and museum. By the end of 1894, he reported that he had a full set of materials from the U.S. Bureau of Education including reports, circulars of information, and histories of education (probably the centennial state histories), and "a most excellent collection of maps." He collected photographs of model classrooms, teachers and students, rural and urban schools, and "noted educators." Among other material in the museum was a collection of "specimens of penmanship, number work, free-hand drawing, map-drawing, pretty [putty?] maps, work in clay, examination papers, and all kinds of school work which can be used as illustration in pedagogical training." Blank forms and specimens of school records, report cards, and class records were on display as well as sets of textbooks for various subjects and grade levels. He insisted that "the value of such collections is plainly evident." He compared the need for an educational museum in training teachers with the necessity of "cabinets of minerals" in training scientists.

In methodology, Karns was a Herbartian, and his course outlines invariably included the five formal steps: perception, apperception, concept, interest, and laws of learning. (Parkham-McCoy, 1929). As was customary at the time, the curriculum relied heavily on textbooks. Karns (1893b) described the junior year in the advanced (degree) program:

> Education doctrine, history, and practice. City-school organization, and supervision. Physical education. Manual training. Textbooks: Payne's School Supervision. DeGarmo's Essentials of Methods.

Classically trained, he also proposed that candidates for a degree in pedagogy should have three years of Latin and two of Greek.

President Charles W. Dabney, the young and energetic proponent of professional studies and later a prominent leader in the southern educational campaigns, gave Karns and the teachers' department strong initial support. But, his enthusiasm waned quickly for reasons that are not clear from extant documents but seem to be related to academic quality and the low standards for entering the program. Karns had few allies from the rest of the faculty. Most had been cold to the idea of becoming involved in teacher education from the beginning. In the previous twenty years, they had allowed two other programs in teacher education to die from lack of nurture. The teachers' department was abolished in 1895, and Karns's title was changed to professor of philosophy and pedagogics. Karns argued that pedagogy should "be taught in a distinct school, or department of the university," but agreed that "for the present" it could become part of the philosophy department (Karns, 1893b).

Karns tried to play on Dabney's sense of the University role as a service institution. "Through the education and professional training of the thousands of instructors whom we may send forth to teach," he wrote Dabney (Karns, 1893b), "our university may become a great power and an instrument for incalculable good." In the new program, Karns attempted to increase academic standards "in order that those who take the degree may meet creditably" the demands of teaching and so that the "foundations of their education may be well laid."

Dabney was on leave from the University in 1896, serving as United States Assistant Secretary of Agriculture. He was still unsatisfied and discussed his continuing reservations with Karns in Atlanta at the World's Cotton Exposition. After successfully negotiating proposed changes with the faculty and trustees, Karns (1893a) wrote to Dabney, "You told me to do as I pleased about the matter. . . . In making these changes I have had in view a compliance with what I thought would be your wishes in the matter." Entrance requirements for those wishing to teach were made the same as for all other students and course work was to be "equal in character" to that done in the other schools. The result, Karns assured Dabney, was to put teacher training on a "higher plane," so that the students in pedagogy would not be "segregated or made different from others." Continuing disagreements with Dabney, however, caused Karns to resign in 1899. He was not replaced, and pedagogy was not taught in the University until 1902 when a new department of education was created under the leadership of Philander P. Claxton.

Karns was not an intellectual and only by the most liberal standards of the time could he be considered a scholar. He wrote two books. *Tennessee History Stories* was written for children in the elementary school. In the "great boys school" of history, it told inspiring tales of good boys doing great deeds. There is no reason to believe that the book's characters much resembled the actual persons of the same name. Neither original research nor scholarly interpretation is found in his book for older persons, *A History of the Politics and Government of Tennessee*.

He was a popular professor. Students and other audiences appreciated him for his humor and repartee. His reputation as a teacher was that he was easy, a bit of an Aunt Polly. A generation after his retirement, a student paper (Parkham-McCoy, 1929) described him as "essentially a simple, earnest soul"; a fair appraisal. His favorite poems, as a case in point, were Longfellow's "The Village Blacksmith" and "The Psalm of Life." His tastes, Baptist faith, and genial personality made him one of the most popular educators in the region. At his death, the Knox County teachers established an educational library as a memorial. Later, a county high school was named for him, and the area surrounding Knox County is called the Karns Community.

## PHILANDER PRIESTLY CLAXTON: CRUSADER FOR PUBLIC EDUCATION IN THE SOUTH

Called, with some justification, the Horace Mann of the South, Philander Priestly Claxton was born in a log cabin on a Tennessee farm in 1862. His parents were strong supporters of schooling although they had limited formal education. His father, a member of the local board of education, had three months of schooling. Claxton attended several "cabin" schools within walking distance, spending three years at "Yaller Cat" school taught by his uncle. He later enrolled in a backwoods academy, where at sixteen he taught classes for a remission of fees. He attended the University of Tennessee on borrowed money. A campus leader, he graduated from the classical curriculum in two and one-half years, second in his class of sixteen (Lewis, 1948).

After graduation, he crossed the mountains to teach in a new elementary school in North Carolina. The other first-year teacher was Edwin Alderman; they became friends and roommates. The school superintendent, E. P. Moses, introduced Claxton to the new science of pedagogy. Thus, early in his career, he became friends with two educators who in the early twentieth century would become leaders in the education campaigns to fund public schools in the South. He began to study educational literature that led to his becoming one of the most articulate leaders among Southern progressives.

After two years of teaching, he decided to attend a "real" university and entered Johns Hopkins, majoring in Teutonic languages. He enrolled in courses taught by J. Franklin Jamison, Herbert Baxter Adams, and Richard T. Ely. He also took a "most inspiring and informational" course in pedagogy from G. Stanley Hall. He immersed himself in the intellectual and cultural life of Baltimore, exciting stuff for a Tennessee farm boy. A six-month trip to Leipzig to study German schools was even more heady: "There are certain streets and restaurants where, I have been told, every other man was a professor, and author or critic more or less well known to fame" (Lewis, 1948, p. 52). He served as a school administrator in several small systems in North Carolina, and from 1893 until 1902 taught pedagogy at North Carolina Normal and Industrial College.

At the turn of the century, President Charles Dabney at the University of Tennessee was intent on making the University the headquarters of the Southern education campaigns. A member of the Southern Education Board, Dabney brought Claxton to Knoxville to head the Board's Bureau of Investigation and Information, the propaganda arm of the movement, and to edit its journal, *Southern Education*. Dabney was convinced, despite his experience with Karns, that pedagogy could be a scholarly pursuit. Both Claxton and Dabney were adept at securing funds from Northern philanthropists, and they soon convinced the interlocking General Education Board (GEB) to finance a department of education at the University that would "rival Chicago and Teachers College, Columbia." They also organized the Summer School of the South with GEB funds, making it the largest summer school in the United States and the source of thousands of workers in the southern educational campaigns. Claxton served as head of the Department of Education and superintendent of the summer school from from 1902 until 1911. During that period, more than 20,000 Southern teachers enrolled, and such distinguished guests as John Dewey, Jane Addams, William T. Harris, and Booker T. Washington spoke—the last in town because Black visitors were not allowed on campus (Allison, 1984).

The Department of Education, under Claxton, was modeled after Columbia's Teachers College, "acknowledged to be the finest of its kind in America" (press release, 1902). The Department depended on financial support from the GEB for its existence. The changing whims of the GEB and misunderstandings about the way the money was to be spent created uneasiness among the faculty. The most injurious blow to the fortunes of the new department fell when Dabney resigned to take the presidency of the University of Cincinnati in 1904. The education faculty, with Dabney's encouragement, left for jobs elsewhere leaving only Claxton, who was tormented for weeks as he decided whether he should accept Dabney's offer to become dean of education at Cincinnati (Claxton, 1905b; 1905c).

Brown Ayres, Dabney's successor, served as president until 1919. A physicist, Ayres had a strong bias against pedagogy; within months of taking office, he wrote to other university presidents asking them about the advisability of teachers colleges in such institutions. After failing to secure additional funding from Northern philanthropists to support the department (Peabody did contribute $500 from his own pocket), Ayres recommended to the University trustees that plans for a practice school be discontinued and that only Claxton's position in education be retained. "Our educational department would have grown very rapidly, and would have been one of the largest in the country," Claxton (1905a) wrote in disgust, had it not been "for the coldness and opposition with which it was received here." Claxton's own position was secure because of his immense popularity with politicians, businessmen, and educators outside the University.

Claxton led a brilliant and successful campaign for state financial support for Tennessee's public schools, culminating in the far-reaching and expensive school law of 1909. During the campaign he spoke in every county in the state and to an estimated 100,000 persons. Some of his speeches lasted for several hours:

> The people in the Southern States were raised on all day camp meetings, and when they go and carry their dinner with them it is an offense to speak a half hour and dismiss them. The man who had come twenty miles to hear a speaking wants to hear a good deal of it (Claxton, 1908a).

The law significantly increased appropriations for public schools, established three normal schools, and provided the first state appropriation for the University of Tennessee.

He campaigned for structural reforms that David Tyack (1974) in *The One Best System* identifies with organizational progressives: the establishment of high schools and kindergarten, school consolidation, pupil transportation, school libraries, "professional" supervision of schools, compulsory attendance, professionally trained teachers, and industrial education.

In the name of democracy, Claxton (1909) was willing to engage in a considerable amount of compulsion. "Old nests of Illiteracy," he argued, "can be broken up only by laws compelling ignorant and indifferent parents to send their children to the schools which the state provides, or to others at least as good." He added that communities that did not provide adequate school buildings and equipment may "need a little of the same brand of compulsion that the parents need."

Throughout his life, he was sure that he knew the best way for others to live. In 1906 he joined the Knox County Saloon League, and much later in the early 1930s he campaigned to retain prohibition. In the 1940s, while president of Austin Peay State College, he would not allow Coca-Cola in the cafeteria because it caused students to waste money that could be spent on wholesome food (Lewis, 1948).

In the Southern educational campaigns, Claxton (1908d) boldly spoke for industrial education—the paramount tenet of orthodoxy in the movement. "It is the idea of the projectors of the campaign for high schools to fit the pupils for work," he insisted, "not for graces." He went on to proclaim that modern society demanded that men work, and a man "who fails to do his part must be made to understand that he is a parasite and entitled to little consideration." The schools must teach, he argued, that "donning overalls and undertaking the task before him," raises rather than lowers a man's status. These quotes are from his speech in support of a particular cause. His own philosophy of education was more balanced and eclectic. In 1911, Lucile Cole (1911) of Mississippi Women's College asked him point-blank which was better, classical or scientific education. Claxton (1911) refused to choose: "They both have their merits." He went on to argue his lifetime position that "it very important in every person's education there should be a good amount of attention to good literature, art and the things pertaining to the cultivation of the imagination, emotions and affections." As U.S. Commissioner of Education from 1911 to 1921, he championed foreign languages and art and music education, subjects sometimes slighted by progressives.

He advocated moral education in public schools and seemed to be unable to entertain the notion that there might be conflict between teaching values derived from a particular religious tradition and religious freedom. He was on the Executive Committee of the Character Education Institution from 1913 to 1921, and he supported the public school work of the Women's Christian Temperance Union and the Young Men's Christian Association.

Recent history is critical of the treatment of Blacks in the Southern education campaigns. At best, the leaders refused to challenge the elaborate doctrine of racial inequality and proposed what Henry Bullock (1967) has called the Great Detour, a special, separate system of industrial schools for Blacks. Claxton's attitude was a typical Southern progressive blend of paternalism towards Blacks, on one hand, and fear and loathing of extreme white bigots on the other. Throughout the campaigns, when he spoke of the education needs of the Southern people, he meant whites. Claxton (1908a) insisted that Blacks would have schools "suited to their racial characteristics and needs" because Southerners "with their blue eyes and soft hearts, can be moved." He branded as "absurd" arguments that schooling spoiled blacks. "It is a very poor school," he retorted, "that does not have better effect on the moral character of the negro than loafing around the slums of a city or in country cross roads places" (Claxton, 1907).

He shared the general Southern whites' hostility to advice on "the Negro Question" from outsiders. To an inquiry from G. Stanley Hall on research concerning Southern Blacks, Claxton (1904a) responded with a short list of publications, including the Atlanta University Studies, and the following observation:

> . . . we people of the South know very little about the negro. What little we do know we have learned from Northern people who have never seen the South, or write learnedly, at least dogmatically, on the subject after having spent two or three days, or probably a week, in this section.

Claxton (1921) approved (as "wise as eloquent") Booker T. Washington's Atlanta Compromise: "In all things purely social, separate as the fingers, yet one as the hand in all things essential to mutual progress." While supporting an increase in the poll tax, Claxton (1904b) claimed that he did not want to disenfranchise Blacks, but wanted to broaden the tax base beyond real estate taxes to increase financial support for schools. A correspondent (Harris, 1908) from Wartrace, Tennessee, asked Claxton for literature or information for a debate on whether "the Constitution should be changed so as to deny all except the Caucasian race a right to vote." The cautious Claxton (1908b) responded that he did not have any information on either side nor did he think the question was "practical" because there was "no possibility of the fifteenth amendment being changed any time soon."

The University of Tennessee had a long tradition of low faculty salaries, and the influential and highly sought after Claxton, never a man to underestimate his worth, presented a special problem. Ayres (1908) took credit for the idea of giving Claxton a double salary so he would be able to remain, paying him both as a regular professor and as a propaganda agent for Tennessee high schools.

A few years later, when the University was in worse than usual fiscal circumstances, Ayres caught wind of the fact that Claxton was receiving yet a third salary as campaign manager of the Southern Education Board. In an angry, four-page letter ("The fact that you have heretofore drawn a double salary has not been uncriticized, but I have in all cases defended it . . ."), Ayres (1908) repeated the rumors about Claxton's large outside salary, and made a blunt request:

I would like to ask you whether this is true and to say that if it is true I think that you should be willing to give up as much of your University salary as you receive from the Southern Education Board, even up to the full amount of the salary.

Throughout his life, Claxton was interested in money and enjoyed living well. He demanded high salaries in job negotiations, refusing the deanship at the University of Cincinnati unless he were to receive "a salary of at least $3,000 a year" (1905b). Claxton (1923) wrote President Morgan that he would not be interested in returning to Tennessee without "assurance" of at least the $7,500 that he was receiving as provost at the University of Alabama. Instead of returning to Tennessee, he became the highest salaried school superintendent in the country when he went to Tulsa for $13,500 in 1923 (Lewis, 1948).

Claxton was one of the best-known peace advocates among educationists. As a young teacher, he despaired of the cost in money and blood of the Philippines Insurrection. A member of the executive committee of the American Peace Society and a founder of the American School of Peace League, he developed a series of lectures for the Carnegie Peace Foundation in 1915. He was a charter member of the League to Enforce Peace, a major lobby for the League of Nations. In his eighties, following World War II, he wrote an antiwar satire, "War for Oldsters Only," in which he advocated settling disputes by old men playing in international golf meets. At ninety, Claxton (1952) proposed a series of "One World Readers" to enable people in all countries ". . . to understand and feel their common humanity and to help toward permanent peace and world cooperation." He developed an elaborate plan by which he would oversee the preparation of the books, and the Ford Foundation would underwrite the cost.

He was the target of an angry attack from the right during World War I. During his tenure as U.S. Commissioner of Education, the Sons of the American Revolution and the *Army and Navy Journal* charged him with distributing pacifist literature at government expense and of belittling the flag in unpatriotic speeches. Upton Sinclair, in *The Goslings*, accused him of being drunk in the streets before such a speech. Claxton seemed fearless before his attackers, generally ignoring them and occasionally correcting a fact. During the war, he further angered his critics by resisting attempts to prohibit the teaching of German (Lewis, 1948): We are "at war with the Imperial Government of Germany and not with the German language or literature" (p. 205). While he was Tulsa superintendent of schools in the 1920s, the *Tulsa World* attempted unsuccessfully to discredit him by resurrecting charges that his pacifism had obstructed the war effort. Years later, acknowledging Claxton's devotion to peace, Senator Estes Kefauver among others led an unsuccessful campaign to have the Nobel Peace Prize awarded to him after World War II.

Claxton was strikingly handsome, and education students, schoolteachers in the Summer School of the South, and influential Northern women who supported the Southern education campaign were "crazy about him." According to Lewis (1948), "he [Claxton] was the handsomest man most of us had ever seen," (p. 76) gushed a student at North Carolina Normal and Industrial. Many corresponded with him for years, expressing not only their professional concerns, but often their personal problems and hurts as well, including complaints about Claxton's failures to respond to their letters and offers of affection; "You look like you didn't care and it hurts so" (Whitson, undated). A 1908 speaking tour in the North, including a speech to the students and faculty of Columbia, was particularly successful with the women in the audiences. "You seemed to have created quite a stir in the ranks of the Southern girls at Teachers College," a friend wrote, and Professor Mari Ruef Hofer (1908) was even fascinated by his educational statistics on Tennessee, "as they fall from your lips like 'spicy bon mots!' fresh from *Paree*."

Claxton was an indefatigable worker. During several periods of his life, he made hundreds of speeches a year, wrote extensively, administered complex institutions and survived on three or four hours of sleep a night. "I only wish there were two or three of me," he complained as he pondered his several roles in the University and in the field (Claxton, 1906). He had at least two "nervous breaks" early in his life, one while he was a student at Johns Hopkins, the other at Tennessee while Ayres was reducing the size and influence of the Department of Education and Dabney was encouraging him to come to Cincinnati. Claxton (1905b) wrote to Dabney to explain his "vacillations," commenting openly on "nervous and mental shock, from which I fear I have not fully recovered. For the first time in my life I am afraid to trust my own decisions." These self-doubts were temporary, and Claxton seemed to enjoy excellent emotional and physical health into advanced old age. He also continued to accept work, particularly writing assignments, which he was unable to keep. While he made no original contribution to scholarship, he was a prolific writer of position papers and opinion columns in journals and pamphlets. In 1897, he founded the North Carolina *Journal of Education*. His *Practical Fonetic Alfabet Drill Book* was popular with elementary teachers early in the century, and he coedited a series of elementary school readers in the same period.

Claxton was a complex personality who left people with quite different impressions. His detractors charged that he was arrogant, conceited, and self-seeking; his admirers found him modest, unselfish, and unassuming. He was a passionate advocate. He was neutral about practically nothing. When asked for information for a college debate on the need for compulsory education in Tennessee, Claxton (1908c) responded, "There is no negative side to the question." He was often aggressive in stating his opinions, yet was an effective lobbyist and back-room negotiator. He was courageous in defending his often unpopular opinions but left little evidence of introspection. Occasional self-doubts might have been more becoming for a scholar but would have been a handicap for Claxton's role as a crusader.

## BENJAMIN O. DUGGAN:
## RURAL PROGRESSIVE

Professor of education from 1922 to 1939 and Tennessee Commissioner of Education from 1935 to 1945, Benjamin O. Duggan started teaching in a one-room school in 1889 when he was twenty. His reminiscences include the typical story of having to "whip the tar out of" the big boys to show who was boss (Duggan, 1943). He served as a principal and superintendent of city schools before becoming State Supervisor of High Schools in Tennessee. When the Department of Rural Education was created at the University in 1922, in an effort to strengthen a school of education which had been academic since Claxton's departure in 1911, Duggan was appointed to head it. Surprisingly, he lacked a college degree. "The future of your position," wrote President Harcourt Morgan (1921) in his letter of appointment, "will be based upon your getting your Bachelor's degree next summer and following with Master's degree as early as possible." He did as requested, taking a Master's degree with his own dean while department head. Duggan (known throughout the state as B. O.) was an excellent choice to head the department. Appointed because of his close relationship to school administrators and teachers, he had extraordinary energy, organizing ability, and barely concealed ambition. He led a rigorous statewide movement to uplift country life and improve rural schools.

Duggan was a progressive. He had an exalted faith in the power of schooling to transform rural life, in the survey as a major instrument to effect change, and in consolidation as the solution to the problems of rural schools. He and Morgan shared, with the national country life movement, a belief in the power of science and technology to uplift the quality of life for country folk, and in the need to replace a narrow fundamentalism in rural churches with a social gospel theology. He seemed to have little fear of imposing his view on the rural populace.

The objectives of Duggan's new department were research, study, and experimentation to "promise more satisfactory conditions in the rural counties of Tennessee with special attention to the improvement of educational, social, and economic conditions"—no small task. The means as well as the objective were typically progressive: efficiency in school administration, curriculum "readjusted" to meet the needs of the rural populace, and the establishment of the rural elementary school as a "community center" (Allison, 1985).

The new Department of Rural Education joined enthusiastically in the progressive mania for conducting surveys. President Morgan's proposal to the university trustees to establish the department listed as its first function: "to study intensively rural school conditions in the State" (Duggan, 1922a). Duggan was unencumbered by a lack of doubts about how country folk ought to live or what their values and their behavior should be. In his work in Appalachia, Duggan (1922b) reported that the local populace was "glad to see us" and that, in a variant on boarding around, he was rarely charged for lodging and food, reducing expenses considerably. Years later, however, in an interview with a Knoxville newspaper, Duggan (1930) told a better tale; he was stunned because of a rumor in the "hollows and ridges" that he was a revenue agent in disguise.

Teaching loads were heavy at Tennessee in the 1920s and 1930s. Even Dean Thackston of the School of Education taught twelve hours per week in 1925. Duggan, because of his supervision of rural surveys, was the only education professor who did not teach any courses. As the enthusiasm for rural uplift waned and the frenzy for surveying quieted by the late 1930s, Duggan was more often on campus teaching courses on educational administration. Still, Frank C. Smith, academic dean (provost) in 1938, inquired into Duggan's teaching load, asking Dean Thackston to respond in detail as to the way Duggan spent his time. Thackston (1938) reported that Duggan had been scheduled for twelve, three-hour courses over the past three quarters, including Saturday courses in the fall and spring. In addition, he was directing two school surveys, eight or ten building surveys at the request of the State Department of Education, and supervising graduate students who were conducting eight additional surveys of elementary school buildings. He was also lobbying the State Legislature for the Tennessee Education Association, including direct "responsibility for the State educational campaign in the Third Congressional District." "I believe you will find this to be a complete outline of Mr. Duggan's work," Thackston concluded, "and that you will understand fully just how he is spending his time for the university." Conspicuously absent from the report was mention of research or writing. The only pieces in the University's "Faculty Publications File" for Duggan are two three-page mimeographed pieces, "Suggestions for Developing a Curriculum Program for the State of Tennessee," January 14, 1931, and "A Program of Action for Tennessee," October 24, 1935.

Duggan was an activist rather than a scholar. He delighted in choosing sides and doing battle. He was always in a fight; "I used to wear out secretaries dictating resignations" (Duggan, 1943). When he was state superintendent, his nickname with the press was "Scrappy." He did not write for publication, but he sent a continuing stream of letters and memoranda to University and state officials campaigning for his views and discrediting his adversaries. He was particularly suspicious of other teacher education institutions in the state and alert to any maneuvers by their leaders to gain influence or students at the expense of the University. He was thin-lipped when reacting to Peabody College and its well-known president, Bruce R. Payne. Following a meeting of the Southern Association of Teacher Training Institutions, he reported to Morgan that the association was organized by Payne, "who absolutely controls it, and dictates all its policies." "All those who took leading parts in the program," he complained, "were alumni of Peabody and subservient to its President" (Duggan, 1924).

The power of the omnipresent church-related colleges to place their alumni in public school principalships irritated Duggan (1931): "They are so intense in their local connections." But the greatest danger was from the state normal schools which, in Duggan's (1932) view, were already scheming to expand their proper mission (to train elementary school teachers) at the expense of the University. "The state has been rioting in an orgy of certification of boys and girls—chiefly girls," he thundered after the legislature decided to allow normal schools to certify teachers for rural county high schools.

Exposing competitors to the University for prestige and power in the state was, in part, a tactic of Duggan in his campaign to protect the College of Education from its enemies in administration and in liberal arts. Within two years after the establishment of the College in

1926, there was talk of demoting it. Duggan (1928b) vigorously lobbied for the College. He was much more outspoken than the dean and the rest of the faculty. He assured President Morgan that public school educators had "manifest confidence" in the College. "Undoubtedly," he argued, "the emasculation of the College of Education will destroy the prestige of the University in the public *school* field." When education was only a department, it had little influence on educational policy, and school administrators and "educational thinkers believed that teacher training was not getting a 'square deal'." The spectre of growing power by the state teachers colleges was raised again. If the college was reduced in rank, the teachers colleges would, he warned, establish departments of secondary education and train the state's high school teachers. His strongest argument was political. The legislature was more sympathetic to the public schools than to the University (a school for rich men's sons). "With reduced emphasis on the professional training of educational leaders," he warned, "the enemies of the University will have a most effective weapon in dealing with the legislature." President Morgan, a former agriculture dean, was not anti-pedagogy and was sympathetic with Duggan's rural education work. The college was saved, at least for a while.

Academic dean and, after 1934, President James D. Hoskins was Duggan's nemesis in the struggle to preserve the College. Irascible and thin-skinned, Hoskins fired education professor Jesse Sprowels in 1923 for insubordination (in part for poking fun at him) and then terminated the contracts of six professors who came to Sprowels's defense, bringing a censure of the University by the American Association of University Professors (Allison, 1983a). In public addresses and in the press, Hoskins was a vigorous campaigner against progressive education and, privately and quietly, against schools of education. In a letter marked *Personal and Confidential* (Hoskins, 1946b) to his strongest supporter on the Board of Trustees, he warned against education professors, "the most aggressive men in education." They had gotten into powerful positions where "they have played havoc, or you might say hell, with the program of education as it is carried on today." When asked about a candidate to replace him as president, Hoskins (1946a) replied that he didn't know the man, but according to *Who's Who* he was a professor of education and "in my opinion, [that] settles it."

In 1932, ostensibly because of redundancy with the work of, and hostility from, the state teachers colleges, Hoskins considered eliminating undergraduate teacher education, which would probably have destroyed the College of Education. Duggan (1932) somewhat fool-hardily called Hoskins's plan "illogical and inexpedient." As a result of the vacillation of the University, "Public education leaders and thinkers," he responded, "will lose faith in the fitness of the University" to train leaders for public schools. Besides, he charged, the real enemies of the College of Education were the liberal arts faculty, not the teachers colleges:

> The most severe and unfair criticism that I have heard, *or heard of* anywhere in the state against professional education in the University of Tennessee has been made on the campus and in the classrooms of the University by members of the University faculty.

Despite Hoskins's misgivings, teacher education managed to survive.

Duggan was vainglorious and ambitious. "Knowing the education situation of the state intimately as I do and the attitude of the principals and superintendents toward the University of Tennessee," he wrote in a typical memorandum to the president, "I cannot see any other course open to the University than as indicated in these suggestions" (Duggan, 1928a). President Morgan received a steady flow of letters from Tennessee's "best people" lauding Duggan and the Department of Rural Education. On occasion, a campaign of support may be suspected. In December 1928, as an example, there was a flood of resolutions, letters, and other testimonials to Morgan from county officials, lawyers, businessmen, and school administrators extolling "the worthiness of the activities of Professor B. O. Duggan." If he had not "taken a hand in affairs in this county the past few years," a high school principal wrote, "Union County [sic] with its bitter political faction [sic] would have regraded [sic] educationally rather than made some remarkable progress as is the case." Without a campaign to solicit support for Duggan, the motivation of the Maynardville lawyer who wrote the following lukewarm letter is obscure:

> I am not familiar with all the work that has been done in this [Union] County by Professor Duggan, but I know that he has spent considerable time in the county, and the work done by him, of which I am familiar, appears to have been well worth while.

Morgan's polite but unenthusiastic replies to the testimonials may indicate that he was aware of the campaign (Testimonials, 1928). In an interview with the *Knoxville Sentinel* on the success of the Union

County survey and subsequent reform campaign, Duggan (1930) engaged in typical false modesty: "While it was my idea, I don't want any credit for what has been done."

Duggan was a publicist and a promoter rather than a scholar. He was more adept at the political processes of institutionalizing change or of protecting institutions than of intellectual inquiry. He was an insightful student of tactics for gaining support for his projects. Duggan (1934) wrote to his predecessor as Tennessee State Commissioner of Education on the difficulties of educational innovation: "Suggestions practical enough to be of value in actual practice often lack sufficient color to be received as sufficiently far reaching to merit or justify special consideration." In a later era, he would have been a superb education grantsman.

## CONCLUSION

In the late nineteenth and early twentieth centuries, Harvard University and the University of Tennessee were a great distance apart in mission and prestige, as they still are. Yet their experiences with professors of pedagogy were similar. As Hazlett notes in the previous chapter, Paul Hanus was not brought to Harvard for his "scholarly potential" but because particular tasks needed to be done, specifically school reform. Similarly, Claxton and Duggan were used at Tennessee to campaign for educational reforms, not to conduct research in or theorize about pedagogy. The University of Tennessee was not a cosmopolitan institution. Southerners, with wives who were Southern "ladies," had a distinct advantage in being employed by the University, although a Yale degree was not considered much of a handicap. The three Tennessee professors of education with their farm upbringing and local bachelor's degrees had more narrow backgrounds than most of the rest of the faculty; only Duggan had an earned Master's degree, and it was from his own department.

As Raths in this volume and others have stated, the education professoriate lives in two cultures—that of the University and that of the public school. The Tennessee professors of education embraced the occupational standard of the public schools. They were practitioner rather than discipline oriented. Claxton in the Southern education campaigns, Duggan in rural community reform, and Karns in the summer institutes received their plaudits from off-campus work.

These men were politically astute. Their strengths were in lobbying, promoting, and administering, where they performed valuable service for the University. They developed allies in school administrators, politicians, and the press. There was a coldness from the liberal arts faculty, and these professors often felt that their positions were endangered. The antipathy of other faculty was not based simply on the paucity of academic credentials, but also on widespread feelings that there was something suspect about pedagogy as a field of study. Karns, Claxton, and Duggan were courageous and, usually, effective defenders of teacher education in the University, but security for their programs and expansion of them depended more on the champions in the president's office than on their own efforts.

These, then, are three case studies of early professors of education at one institution. Like most case studies, they supply detailed information and suggest anomalies. They represent the building blocks of a history of the professors of teaching. When more such studies are available, generalizations can be more confidently drawn. In essence, they show the raggedness of reality.

Many of the historical and contemporary generalizations about education professors are supported by an examination of three professors in different generations in one place. Although we have biographies of famous professors at prestigious institutions, we lack sketches of more ordinary professors of education (but not so ordinary that they left no record of their activities) in more modest schools of education. One purpose of history is to help us find ourselves in the past. Most of us who are professors will not recognize ourselves as Harold Rugg at Teachers College, but we may see ourselves as Benjamin O. Duggan of Tennessee.

## REFERENCES

All documents, including letters, letterbooks, memoranda, class papers, speeches and manuscripts used in these references may be found in Special Collections, Hoskins Library, The University of Tennessee, Knoxville.

Allison, C. (1983). The University of Tennessee faculty controversy of 1923. *Proceedings of the Twenty-Third Annual Meeting of the Southwestern Philosophy of Education Society, 33*, 107–13. (a)

_____ (1983). Training Dixie's teachers: The University of Tennessee's Summer Normal Institutes. *Journal of Thought, 18*(3), 27–36. (b)

_____ (1984). The summer school of the South. *Proceedings of the Twenty-Third Annual Meeting of the Southwestern Philosophy of Education Society, 34*, 194–201.

_____ (1985, November). *The country life movement in Tennessee: Educationists and rural reform.* Paper presented at the Meeting of the History of Education Society, Atlanta.

Ayres, B. (August 25, 1980). Letter to P. Claxton.

Bullock, H. (1967). *A history of Negro education in the South.* New York: Praeger Publishers.

Claxton, P. (December 9, 1904). Letter to G. Hall. (a)

_____ (December 9, 1904). Letter to J. Wright. (b)

_____ (January 16, 1905). Letter to M. Hofer. (a)

_____ (May 23, 1905). Letter to C. Dabney. (b)

_____ (June 12, 1905). Letter to C. Dabney. (c)

_____ (November 17, 1906). Letter to M. Hofer.

_____ (February 23, 1907). Letter to H. Summer.

_____ (1908). *Proceedings of the Eleventh Conference for Education in the South,* p. 79. (a)

_____ (March 17, 1908). Letter to I. Harris. (b)

_____ (April 7, 1908). Letter to C. Ruch. (c)

_____ (February 2, 1908). Quoted in *Nashville America.* (d)

_____ (1909) Campaign speech. (Ms. No. 278)

_____ (January 21, 1911). Letter to L. Cole.

_____ (1921). *University of Tennessee Record.* p. 11.

_____ (June 20, 1923). Letter to H. Morgan.

_____ (1952). Analysis of purposes, plans and means for "One World Reader." Unpublished paper.

Cole, L. (January 18, 1911). Letter to P. Claxton.

Dabney C. (July 29, 1896). Letterbook.

Duggan, B. (1922). Education and economic survey of Union County. Unpublished paper. (a)

_____ (October 23, 1922). Letter to H. Morgan. (b)

_____ (October 24, 1924). Letter to H. Morgan.

_____ (July 23, 1928). Letter to H. Morgan. (a)

_____ (July 31, 1928). Letter to H. Morgan. (b)

_____ (August 26, 1930). Quoted in *Knoxville News Sentinel*.

_____ (January 15, 1931). Letter to J. Thackston.

_____ (March 21, 1932). Letter to J. Hoskins.

_____ (November 15, 1934). Letter to W. Cocking.

_____ (August 1, 1943). Quoted in *Nashville Tennessean*.

Greene, M. (1973). Identities and contours: An approach to educational history. *Educational Researcher, 2*, 5–10.

Harris, I. (March 13, 1908). Letter to P. Claxton.

Hofer, M. (February 11, 1908). Letter to P. Claxton.

Hoskins, J. (August 28, 1946). Letter to P. Kruesi. (a)

_____ (October 18, 1946). Letter to P. Kruesi. (b)

Karns, T. (February 18, 1893). Letter to C. Dabney. (a)

_____ (May 29, 1893). Letter to C. Dabney. (b)

_____ (1894). Report of the Teachers' Department. *University of Tennessee Biennial Report*.

Lewis, C. (1948). *Philander Priestly Claxton: Crusader for public education*. Knoxville, Tenn.: The University of Tennessee Press.

Morgan, H. (October 3, 1921). Letter to B. Duggan.

Of Local Interest. (1894). *Tennessee University Magazine, 6*, 42–43.

Parham-McCoy, M. (1929). *Two East Tennessee Educators*. Unpublished term paper.

Press Release. (1902). University of Tennessee.

*Testimonials*. (1928). A number of letters in praise of Duggan. Archives 4, Box 47.

Thackston, J. (March 19, 1938). Letter to F. Smith.

Tyack, D. (1974). *The one best system*. Cambridge, Mass.: Harvard University Press.

Whitson, D. (undated). Letter to P. Claxton. (Ms. No. 278)

Wolff, G. (1979). Minor lives. In M. Pachter (Ed.), *Telling lives: The biographer's art* (pp. 56–72). Washington, D.C.: New Republic Books.

*Author's Note:* Much of the material on Claxton's early life is from Lewis' (1948) work.

# 4

# The New Priorities and the Education Faculty

## MILTON SCHWEBEL

### INTRODUCTION

Research universities are determined to achieve improvements, as measured by knowledge productivity, among all disciplines. No discipline is exempt from pressures to focus on research and scholarship; none free of the sanctions that make the pressures irresistible.

Faculties in education, once ignored, now are much in the limelight. The reactions to being in this relatively new position fall at the extremes, with some professors of education experiencing it as being "under the gun," and others considering it an opportunity to bring about overdue changes in the role definition of education faculty. One expectation is very clear: only those education faculty whose research and scholarly publications help elevate the status of the school or department should receive tenure. The goal is to narrow the gap between similar units nationally as well as between more illustrious departments on campus.

Anyone who values new knowledge must support the goal of raising the quality and quantity of research of education faculties. Research and scholarly activity are as essential to the vitality of a professional school as to that of the arts and sciences units. They are important not simply because universities value them, but in their own right to achieve profound understanding of development, learning, and teaching. They are important, also, to assure the society that what occurs in the classrooms of America's schools is the best possible, the product of the most advanced thinking.

This chapter addresses the implications of the changes in progress. It is based on two prime assumptions: first, that education faculty are becoming something different from what they have been almost since the inception of American teacher education; second, that the direction of change is irreversible. The past is dead. To bemoan that fact may be useful for dealing with personal frustrations but for little else. Whether dissatisfied or not, education faculty and faculties of all disciplines, academic administrators, public policymakers and the public at large—all in their own interest—urgently need to consider the contemporary and future consequences of the changes discussed. In this chapter, several obvious consequences of the two most important changes are examined: the rise in status to unchallenged primary position of the research/scholarship role; the decline of the teaching role to secondary or tertiary position; and the growing isolation of education faculty from the schools, the source of professional nourishment in the past (see Author's Note, 1).

## ACADEMIC ROLES

The university, in its long history, has given faculties the dual roles of the *reproduction* and *production* of knowledge. The educational reproduction function was paramount during the early period and much of the history of the institution. Beginning late in the last century in Germany, the production role became increasingly prominent and has become paramount in the United States in the last twenty-five years (Touraine, 1974).

In the reproduction role, universities serve the social order in several significant ways. They help select and educate the national elite that maintains and perpetuates the social order. The universities propagate the establishment's ideology, provide it with the skills of leadership, and train the hierarchy of technical and managerial cadres essential to carrying out the dictates of leadership. Among those cadres are the thousands of education faculty whose function is to prepare the hundreds of thousands of teachers who provide schooling to the millions of children who will later fill positions in factory, office, and countless service occupations.

The marked tipping of the scale in the direction of the production role was not a historical accident, as the French sociologist and educator Touraine explained in his study of the American academic system. After World War II, the advanced, industrialized societies began to rely increasingly on science to the point that the production function became indispensable. It became critical when the rivalry between the United States and Russia sharpened in the post-Sputnik era. According to Touraine (1974), science itself constitutes the cultural model of society in the United States. Economic circumstances compel universities to be compatible with the cultural model, for otherwise there would be no incentive for the society to withhold resources from other productive uses and assign them to educational institutions. Universities are supported with the expectation that society will benefit through enhancement of the national economy. Economic growth and knowledge production are interrelated. While they have varied functions, the American universities' prime function is the production of knowledge.

## STATUS OF EDUCATION FACULTY

In the 1920s as education faculty first joined the university in substantial numbers with the assignment to "reproduce" vast numbers of teachers, the assignment of other faculties, especially in science, was to become more heavily productive. After World War II, when the production function accelerated, education faculty prepared thousands of teachers for the first postwar population bulge. Consequently, in the academic community, two cultures emerged and diverged from a single point. Later in this volume, Raths and associates comment in a similar vein. This difference persisted at least until the decline in teacher demand about fifteen years ago, when moves toward convergence began.

The years of the mass reproduction role are clearly evidenced by education faculty. In proportion to faculty size, education faculty had more graduates at the master's and doctoral level than seven other fields. They had a less favorable faculty-student ratio than others. This finding, combined with another in the same study (Schwebel, 1982), shows the disadvantages under which education faculty operated in respect to opportunity for research and scholarship. Compared with other disciplines, education professors reported approximately equivalent number of both total work hours and those hours devoted to teaching, preparation, and counseling. Professors in other fields, however, reported spending 22 percent of their time in research and scholarly writing, compared to the education faculty's 10 percent; the education faculty reported giving 31 percent of their time to administration in contrast to the other professors' 14 percent. At least one-half of the time professors in the biological and social sciences and agriculture were busy with research and writing; education faculty were engaged in administrative matters. That is a substantial difference in time allocation for role performance.

Despite heavier student loads and additional administrative assignments, education faculty's publication productivity, measured quantitatively, is remarkably close to that of arts and sciences faculties. Two studies found marked similarity between the number of publications of education faculty and faculties from other disciplines, although one study reported a smaller proportion of empirical studies by education faculty (Ducharme & Agne, 1982; Schwebel, 1982). A qualitative measure would be preferable, but the quantitative standard should not be disparaged. It is questionable that Shakespeare and Beethoven would be honored if they had produced only one or two works, even if these had been *Hamlet* and the Fifth Symphony, respectively. Quantity is a necessary, although not sufficient criterion.

These comparisons were made after attempts at convergence were already begun. The earliest efforts, which date back about twenty-five years, were largely limited to a relatively small number of institutions. Universities that followed suit did so in the intervening years, some five or ten years ago; others are only now struggling to convert to a research-oriented status.

## CONVERGENCE EFFECTS ON EDUCATION FACULTY

With an alteration of schools of education of such great magnitude—a reversal of fundamental priorities—one anticipates a variety of effects. The number of courses taught and students encountered are reduced. Graduate programs achieve even higher status because specialized, advanced graduate courses more closely reflect the research interests of professors. Graduate students serve as paid or unpaid research assistants; undergraduate courses lose whatever appeal they may have had because they offer little apparent reward to faculty in research-oriented institutions. The new values may even lessen the impact of student course evaluations, whereas the number of papers published and the prestige of the journals in which faculty appear become even more significant.

In this process, education faculty increasingly look for respect and admiration from university peers and administrators rather than from school personnel. Schools and teachers recede into the background. To the extent that professorial research requires elementary or secondary school students as subjects, a matter dictated in part by priorities of funding agencies, connections with school systems must be maintained. The connections, however, are different from the past when the professor observed student-teachers, mingled with cooperating teachers, and felt affiliated with both the public schools and the university. Many faculty conduct little or no research in schools, at least not the kind that requires an ongoing association with teachers and students. Education faculty in research universities, those that have achieved their aim to be in conformity with other disciplines and those en route to that position, should have high esteem on their own campus and in the academic community at large. Faculty in institutions that cannot or do not attempt to transform themselves drop further in status.

These are suppositions writ large about the effects of the ongoing transformations of schools of education. Harry Judge found that graduate schools of education in America's elite research universities had indeed succeeded in making the transformation (Judge, 1982). If undergraduate education had been a prior responsibility, it no longer was; or it was retained because of pressure from arts and sciences faculty who needed a "dumping ground" and who recognized the importance to their self-interest of numbers of students and credit hours. The continuation of undergraduate programs represents no burden to education faculty because it is often their teaching assistants, not they themselves who teach the courses. Further, education faculty get a bonus in that the assistantships attract talented graduate students. While many arts and sciences professors, and even education faculty, have no respect for undergraduate education courses and the students who take them, nearly all tolerate them as necessary evils. At the graduate level, even the master's students were not particularly valued except for the fact that, having reduced or eliminated their involvement with undergraduates, faculty required a mass source of graduate credit hours in order to afford what they seek most, a cadre of highly select doctoral students. Teaching was, at best, secondary, if not pushed out of even that position by consultation for governmental agencies or corporations; research activity was, of course, at the pinnacle.

But what kind of research? Much of it, according to Judge (1982), has little direct relationship to teacher education. The areas of interest and the problems addressed emerge more from the literature of the behavioral sciences than from the work environment of teachers and students. The role of education faculty in teacher education is, at best, to *study* it but most emphatically not to *work* in it. The extent to which education faculty investigators choose topics significant to the real world of the classroom depends on their perspicacity despite the fact they are not part of that world and, out of necessity if not personal preference, tend to distance themselves from it.

Because they are removed from the schools, productive education faculty are psychologically as well as physically distant from those expected to utilize the knowledge they produce. What happens to the product of research is indicative of the developing pyramid in the role of types of institutions of higher education with regard to teacher education and schools. Judge refers to two hypothetical professors who "create knowledge" and propagate it through their students, their books, and the publications of other professors and teachers. The best of their students will teach elsewhere and will, thereby, transmit knowledge produced by their mentors. The latter will reach wider audiences, not only through their own books but, more broadly, through second-order textbooks, the kind used in the education, training and continued education of teachers.

> What is striking about it [this model] is the hierarchical view of dissemination, as well as the apparent distancing of the 'real' world of practitioners or even of students who are to be educated/trained as practitioners. At one level, the model reads like the application of an 'arts and sciences' model to the working of a professional school (Judge, 1982, p. 13).

The outcome of the conversion is unquestionable, as Judge sees it. Removed from the life of schools for children, the graduate schools of education in the elite research universities are at the apex of professional education, having, in fact, no superiors in "the international business of Education . . ." (Judge, 1982, p. 5).

Judge's observations imply that education faculty will feel comfortable and secure in those institutions. Judge expected these internationally renowned schools to be "assured (and) unassailable" in their position. Yet, he found them to display "alarming symptoms of insecurity and self-doubt . . . their position . . . is always ambiguous and often resented" (Judge, 1982, pp. 5–6). Having distanced themselves from teachers, students, and the gritty problems of the schools, education faculty in elite universities waffle between an arts and sciences and a professional faculty identity. In resolving this ambiguity, they get no help from teachers and administrators who regard their work as irrelevant, and little from liberal arts faculty who still see them cloaked in the inferior garb of educationists.

In many respects, the status of the education faculty in the foremost universities is similar to that of education faculty elsewhere, especially in other universities. Their prestige is low; as a group, they are tolerated rather than respected; the contradictions imposed upon them by trying to live in two incompatible communities pose the threat of occupational schizophrenia. None of this is to suggest that the education faculty in elite universities are to be pitied. They have the very decided advantage of being on top of the pile, even if from the vantage point of the academic tower it is not an appealing pile. Yet, there is nothing appealing about having to "look up" to one's supposed peers in the academic community. Or, at the same time, in "looking down" at those in the schools to receive sneerful expressions about the impotence of their research.

The convergence of priorities in schools of education toward compatibility with those of the university is well under way, with research and scholarship at the pinnacle. The results of the change are not trivial. Knowledge is being produced through highly sophisticated studies by well-trained education faculty. Not rooted in the schools, they obtain their ideas increasingly from behavioral science's literature than from the world of the school. From that mix of sources comes research essentially irrelevant to the relentless educational realities. And the perception of nonrelevance leads with ever more force toward the unhealthy separation of education faculty from the schools.

## BRIDGING THE GAP BETWEEN EDUCATION FACULTY AND THE SCHOOLS

One feels compelled to inquire whether the breach between education faculty and the schools is irreparable. Surely, there must be some way to bridge the difference. Granted, the challenge posed is enormously difficult; the prescription, deceptively simple. Educators must produce something that works and makes life more bearable for teachers. They must help find ways of organizing schools and classes and of teaching students that are more effective. Such activities, however hard to realize, would reduce the barrage of charges against the educational institutions and their personnel.

Practitioners of education want no more than what others have received. They would like the advantage that their counterparts in medicine and dentistry have been given in the last five decades: educational equivalents of antibiotics, fluoride, air drills, laser beams, and the like, and, equally important, a holistic approach to health.

The obvious differences between education and the health fields, with the latter so heavily—although not exclusively rooted in the natural sciences—are not sufficient to justify the relatively limited developments in education. Just what should have or could have been accomplished in the science of education in the past five decades cannot be defined, for prior to experimentation there is no way of knowing the possibilities for advances in a given field during a given period of time. However, it is equally true that those possibilities will never be determined if the most serious problems are systematically avoided. If the issues that matter the most are ignored, then at best only insignificant gains are possible.

The Indian educational researcher, Shib K. Mitra (1974), believes that American educational research has been constricted by its tendency to imitate the physical sciences. As a result, it is indeed a case of the tail wagging the dog. His meaning is clear: problems are chosen not first and foremost in terms of their importance, but rather their suitability for study by the scientific method. By equating acceptable research methodology with statistical thinking, the field has excluded the most complex and significant issues. "In the field of education, one would like to see a systematic study of significant problems rather than a scientific study of insignificant problems" (p. 234).

Membership in a low-status field makes education professors acutely susceptible to the blandishments of measurement (with its appearance of rigor and its status of respectability), so that the most quantifiable problems with variables most easily controlled get preference, whereas those less measurable are shunted aside. This often results in preference for micro-type problems and neglect of the complex web of interacting forces that operate in the ecology of schools. In producing more micro-level, particularistic studies, faculty are doing more than constricting their own range of exploration. They are also educating their graduate students about what is valued in the educational community. The study of micro-level problems is likely to yield the rewards of publication in respectable journals, approval of peers in education if not elsewhere, and tenure.

There is an even more insidious consequence than neglect of important problems. By distancing themselves from the real life of the school, education faculty do not experience the psychological closure that comes from witnessing their product applied in socially useful ways. They suffer the incompleteness of the cobbler whose shoes are not purchased and worn, the artist whose paintings are unseen, the composer whose music is never played. Not only is this the basis for alienation from the community one is supposed to serve; it is the basis for personal alienation and the denial of self-fulfillment.

More than a decade has passed since Mitra's ideas were published, and during that time educational research has flourished more than ever. Each new cohort of education faculty has brought a higher level of sophistication to the task. To ascertain whether significant problems are being currently ignored, one must be able to define "significance" in that context. For purposes of a minuscule assessment, several criteria were employed in the review of two issues (Spring and Fall 1985) of the *American Educational Research Journal* (AERJ).

Two questions were addressed. The first asked whether the problem and study design in each article were such as to make it possible to translate the results into usable findings in the classroom. Thirty percent of the ten articles in the Spring 1985 issue met the criteria, and 44 percent of the nine in the Fall 1985 issue. In making judgments about the adequacy of these percentages, no norms are available for simple application. It seems, however, as far as classroom applicability in this one leading publication is concerned, the situation is not as serious as Mitra pictured it. Some educational researchers are doing studies immediately useful to the school principal and classroom teacher.

This favorable condition raised other issues. When useful results are obtained, systematic methods of incorporating them into the practices of schools and colleges are essential, for otherwise the research represents simply an academic exercise. This in itself becomes an enormously difficult task because, as Judge observed, the research faculty in education who study the real life of the school (reflected, let us say, in the 30 percent and 44 percent of the articles in the two issues) are not part of the school in the same way as their predecessors of several generations ago. They are not in a position of physical presence, close professional relationship and trust to be able to help convert the research findings into classroom practices.

The second question applied to these two issues of the *AERJ* was: How many articles dealt with significant contemporary problems; e.g., illiteracy, low achievement, dropouts, disinterest, drug use in school, and what to do about them. No studies of this kind were found. One can only speculate about the reason for their absence. Mitra would attribute their absence to the fact that these major problems are not conducive to the use of controlled studies of the traditional sort. In any event, Mitra's criticism about the failure to address the most significant problems seems to apply, at least on the basis of an examination of a small sample of papers in this reputable journal.

The critical comments about the "iconization" of the methods of physical science are not to suggest that Mitra was opposed to quantification or to studies that employ statistical designs. He stressed the fact that critical thinking ought not be equated with statistical thinking. Most of all he urged that the tail (methodology) should not wag the dog; that is, determine the choice of the problem. Regrettably, this principle is not an easy one to follow. Conditioned for many years to imitate the physical sciences and to be rewarded accordingly, one can not easily adopt a different frame of reference in defining the nature or characteristics of legitimate research. That is one reason for difficulty in attacking the most perplexing and significant educational problems. There are still other constraints that keep education faculty either remote from studying those problems or, having studied them, having the interest or opportunity to see that the results are applied in the classroom. These other constraints may be more powerful even than that already discussed and may be partly responsible for its existence.

Within a university, the various components do not all serve the same constituencies in the national population. As explained elsewhere (Schwebel, 1985), in both the reproduction and production roles, the arts and sciences faculties and the education faculty have different constituencies. The student body of arts and sciences faculties, and of some professional faculties as well, is composed of future leaders and managers in business and government. The research of those faculties is attuned to the needs of government and the economy. Education faculty, by contrast, have as the bulk of their students those who will serve as teachers to the multitudes who will become factory workers, word processor operators, or unemployment statistics. Educational research is presumably directed toward the problems of educating students who will educate the broad mass of young people.

The distinction between the clientele served has become further accentuated. At about the time that schools of education began transforming themselves into research-oriented institutions, another process in the country was moving at a quickened pace. An automated, computerized society was resulting in a growing shortage of jobs in heavy industry. The portion of the population that had no place to go, no future as participants in the social order was increasing in size. This development created many problems, some of the most complex being those related to the education of the children in that sector of the population.

Society has charged education faculties with the reproduction of the broad mass of young people and production of knowledge to solve the problems of education. In that connection one might ask: *Whose* problems are the schools' problems? The question implies that the significant problems of the schools affect some sectors of the population much more than others. The answer is obvious. A major educational difficulty in the United States, and in other nations, is the schooling of children of the lower social classes, which include a preponderance of disadvantaged minority groups. Virtually all children in public and parochial and many private schools, including privileged children, suffer the effects of ill-advised educational goals and teaching methods that put the highest premium on the information and skills assessed on achievement tests. This contention is powerful since it claims that insufficient attention is paid to facilitating cognitive development, providing opportunity for independent learning and discovery, encouraging critical thinking, and developing "executive" or meta-cognitive (self-controlling, self-regulating) skills (Meichenbaum, 1986).

These enviable goals, usually realized in select private schools, are not likely to be established in other schools, except perhaps in the rhetoric of politicians or the wishful thinking of administrators. At the same time, parents, educators, and school policymakers are not clamoring for the kinds of educational changes that would incorporate these as explicit and realizable goals. Furthermore, assessments of schools typically do not include these goals as criteria of effectiveness. Schools are deemed effective when the drop-out rate is low, achievement test scores are high, and college admission rates, especially admission to competitive institutions, are favorable. Insofar as schools with large proportions of economically lower-income populations are concerned, those goals are impossibly distant. For those schools, simply to keep children in school, to maintain order necessary for instruction, to give students incentives to learn, and to help them concentrate and study are demanding enough, and sometimes beyond the capacity of such schools. These, the most complex educational problems of our time, are inextricably bound to other factors beyond the school (e.g., labor market conditions), over which education faculty and school personnel have no control.

In the past, improvements in education occurred when the national economy demanded higher-level intellectual skills. Usually, this followed a long campaign to gain those advances (e.g., free elementary or high school education) but coincided with recognition of the industrial necessity for them. With an economy that no longer requires the labor of millions of adults and older teenagers, the impulse to expend large resources required to enable them to achieve at a mastery level may not be strong. In terms of sheer economic necessity, there is no purpose in investing heavily in those children who will never have opportunity to enter the labor force which has no room for them and who will therefore wind up on welfare rolls.

Studies of per capita support for education show that the society pays well for what it values most, that is, quality education in private and upper-middle-class suburban schools to reproduce its business and government leadership, its professions, and its knowledge producers. It pays what it must to reproduce the rest of the working force in the more than 30,000 occupations that keep the economy and society moving in gear. It pays least of all to help those at the bottom of the social hierarchy. The contradiction between economic necessity and human need creates a tangled web of problems which stands then as a legacy to teachers and education faculties and others as well.

Education faculty are confronted with an overwhelming challenge: train the teachers and generate the knowledge necessary to educate all the children, including those who are destined to fall into the large category of the futureless population. To use Touraine's terminology again, one function of education faculty is to reproduce the teachers who will reproduce the social classes that attend public school, including members of the class destined to live the demoralizing life of unemployment and welfare support. The other role is to produce the know-how to achieve this end.

Mitra's criticism that educational researchers engage in sophisticated research about not very significant problems can be seen in a new light. The temptation to ignore those problems is great. The possibility of bringing about noticeable change seems remote; the difficulties in experimenting with programs intended to achieve change seem overwhelming; the time required to give such programs a fair test seems unduly long; and the resources necessary to engage in vast projects seem not easily available. These are reasons aplenty to avoid them. In doing so, however, education faculty are doomed to be failures in connection with the most troubling of education's problems.

This is the quandary facing education faculty: to perhaps become mired in finding ways to make the schools work for larger proportions of children, or to follow a safer, more traditional academic path. If education faculty are to "make it" under the new priorities in the university, and if their research is to be useful to the schools, they must choose the riskier course. Those risks are considerably lessened when the federal and state governments demonstrate through investment their interest in change. At times when interest has been exhibited, education faculty (and other faculty) have responded. The result has been important programmatic developments like Head Start, Follow Through (Datta, 1986), and Mastery Learning (Bloom, 1976).

## CONCLUSION

American universities after World War I began the process of reversing priorities. The production of new knowledge began to overtake the reproduction role, so that research became the hallmark of leading universities, a pattern followed later by less distinguished institutions. For education faculty, however, the reproduction role was their hallmark, imposed upon them at least as much by circumstances in the nation and on campus as by professional choice. Not until after World War II, and especially not until the 1960s, did the conversion process toward greater emphasis on the production role begin. This movement for education faculty has, on the positive side, considerably raised the level of research and scholarship. On the negative side, it has led to distancing from schools, questionable relevance of topics investigated, and limited usefulness of results. As a consequence of these factors, uncertainties have developed about the quality of educational programs used in reproducing teachers and other educational personnel.

Assuming, as is the case here, that the new priorities are here to stay, the challenge for education faculty can be stated in question form: How, under the new conditions, can we establish authenticity and credibility? How can we define and engage in studies with benefits for all children, adolescents and adults, including those most in need? What theories, and what research and evaluation methodologies are suitable to contemporary problems? Such questions more than any others define the productive and reproductive roles of education faculty as the twentieth century approaches its end. Answers to those questions must be found. Otherwise, education faculties themselves will become irrelevant. That such answers have been found in the recent past (when notable advances were developed, as in the case of Follow Through) is evidence that they can be found again.

To avoid irrelevance, education faculty, joining with others, have little choice but to pursue the search for new answers. That is the only choice not only when political climate supports them, but at other times as well.

## REFERENCES

Bloom, B. S. (1976). *Human characteristics and school learning*. New York: McGraw-Hill Book Company.

Datta, L. (1986). Benefits without gains: The paradox of the cognitive effects of early childhood programs and implications for policy. In M. Schwebel & C. A. Maher (Eds.). *Facilitating cognitive development: International perspectives, programs, and practices* (pp. 103–126). New York: Haworth Press.

Ducharme, E., & Agne, R. (1982). The education professoriate: A research-based perspective. *Journal of Teacher Education, 33*, 30–36.

Judge, H. (1982). *American graduate schools of education: A view from abroad*. New York: Ford Foundation.

Meichenbaum, D. (1986). Meta-cognitive methods of instruction: Current status and future prospects. In M. Schwebel & C. M. Maher (Eds.), *Facilitating cognitive development: International perspectives, programs, and practices* (pp. 23–31). New York: Haworth Press.

Mitra, S. K. (1974). A brief note on American education research. *American Educational Research Journal, 11*, 41–47.

Schwebel, M. (1982). Research productivity of education faculty: A comparative study. *Educational Studies, 13*, 224–239.

_____ (1985). The clash of cultures in academe: The university and the education faculty. *Journal of Teacher Education, 36,* 2–7.

Touraine, A. (1974). *The academic system in American society.* New York: McGraw-Hill Book Company.

*Author's Note:* (1) Portions of this chapter include adaptations of material in Schwebel, M. (1985).

———————————————————————— 5

# Professors of Education: Uneasy Residents of Academe

EDWARD R. DUCHARME
RUSSELL M. AGNE

## INTRODUCTION

In his chapter, Allison presents a detailed picture of early professors
of education at the University of Tennessee. His portraits demonstrate
that certain issues have deep roots, such as debates regarding theory
and practice, the proper role of education professors in higher education, and so on. Against this background and Hazlett's assertion
that we have no history, we describe some characteristics of contemporary faculty at schools, colleges, and departments of education
(SCDEs), and suggest implications of these characteristics. Obviously, neither the characteristics nor the implications aptly describe
or apply to all professors of education.

Almost anything one says about the professoriate describes some professors, while nothing one says describes all professors. Yet there is need to explore the backgrounds and experiences of professors of education for the value attendant from rigorous self-scrutiny, particularly for a group as poorly known as SCDE faculty.

The information and the viewpoints offered come from two sources: our review of the literature and the data from our ongoing study. Since 1981, we have been collecting and analyzing data on professors of education. We submitted a thirty-nine-item questionnaire to the total SCDE faculty at thirty-two institutions; the return rate of questionnaires has consistently been close to 70 percent. We currently have information on nearly 1,200 professors of education in these institutions. The institutions include at least one in each of the following categories: East Coast state university, Southwestern liberal arts college, Far West state university, historic Black institution, Southwestern university, Midwestern state university, former state teachers college now a university, and a Southern regional university. The most recent survey (Ducharme & Agne, 1987) included all institutions with professional education programs within a single state, ranging from private, four-year liberal arts colleges to the major state university. The study will continue with in-depth interviews with education faculty at a number of these institutions.

The thesis of this chapter is that SCDE faculty behavior is greatly influenced by their personal and professional backgrounds. These backgrounds generally include: lower-middle- and middle-class origins, attendance at nonelitist, four-year state colleges; lack of family experience in higher education; work in the lower schools; part-time study at both the master's and doctorate levels; and pragmatic dissertations or doctoral projects. These characteristics are sometimes reflected in schizophrenic behavior with respect to higher education roles, slow adaptation to higher education norms, a preference for practice over theory, and a distrust of research. In addition to the qualities enumerated above, the education professoriate is overwhelmingly white and male.

We occasionally receive rebukes for our work. Some argue that the conditions we describe are less severe than we suggest, that there are already enough critics of SCDE faculty without criticism from within. We believe SCDE faculty must fill the major role in the preparation of educational professionals within the academy. They cannot fill this role as long as their presence and contributions are suspect. Our work only suggests what must occur for SCDE faculty to assume their proper place in higher education.

Probably every SCDE campus has faculty members whose back-grounds and behaviors contrast with those described or implied here. That is, they are not intimidated by higher education; they conduct high-quality research and publish the results in reputable journals; they value research activities and results; they are active in campus committees and related activities; they contribute to the growth of new knowledge and effective practice and are aware of others' activities in knowledge generation and practice. Our research suggests that such faculty are clearly in the minority.

For some, these observations may appear excessively determin-istic. Why should education faculty behave or be seen as behaving so much in response to their social origins, their early work lives, and the perceptions others have of them? Ought not education to have liberated them from this seemingly preordained behavior pattern? Are SCDE faculty not, in fact, individuals who passionately advocate education as the process whereby individuals are liberated from their pasts? Why should their educations not have liberated them? Lanier (1986) makes the point that early experiences and influences have potency in the prolongation of problems.

> Historical research also supports the idea that low status, hum-
> ble social origins, and low-level knowledge and skills are re-
> lated, and it emphasizes the longevity and tenacity of the
> problem for teacher education. . . . Evidence suggests that
> the typical lineage of teacher educators has not prepared
> them to appreciate the traditional values of higher education
> (pp. 532–33).

## SOCIAL AND EDUCATIONAL BACKGROUNDS

The campus may be a problematical environment for many professors of education. This is not to say that they do not like the environment; rather, the match between their behaviors and the institutional norms is often not a close one; the mismatch may be a result of social and economic backgrounds of professors of education as well as their earlier enculturation in the lower schools.

Fuller and Bown observed (1975):

> Teacher educators, have, by and large, humble social-class ori-
> gins and low status in comparison with their academic col-
> leagues. They more often hold paying jobs while working

toward a degree, enter the faculty later, perhaps with the Ed.D., and so are less likely to have acquired the scholarly credentials valued by academicians (p. 29).

Our studies confirm that Fuller and Bown's observations about the social origins of teacher educators apply to professors of education generally.

Sixty-eight percent of the fathers of professors in our study held positions for which a college education was not the norm, for example, farming. In fact, only 12.6 percent graduated from college, a low incidence of individuals holding college degrees in the home environment. Furthermore, more than 50 percent of those fathers holding college degrees were teachers. The mothers of those in the study were more likely to have completed high school (72 percent to 65 percent, but no more likely to have completed college (12.6 percent to 11.9 percent). Thus, the future SCDE faculty members would have encountered few college graduates other than their own teachers; those few parents having college degrees were often teachers themselves.

These observations suggest a variety of interpretations. One is that future SCDE faculty lack knowledge of what one "did" with a college education beyond teach. The motivations for some students who became teachers, while perhaps including altruism, were based on limited experience, knowledge, and sophistication; in brief, the students were parochial.

Measurements of parochialism are difficult, but indicators are somewhat easier to discern. The presence or absence of a college degree, the nature of studies undertaken, and the distance from home of the college one attended might be indicators of parochialism. Nearly 60 percent of those in our study went no further away from home than 100 miles; 75 percent went no further than 300 miles; only 12 percent went further than 1,000 miles. Finally, 30 percent went no further than twenty-five miles, a situation suggesting that many were nonresident students as undergraduates. Lortie (1975) demonstrated that teachers, more often than not, attend local colleges and teach in areas close to where they grew up. Hence, it is not surprising that professors of education, most of whom taught in the public schools for some time, become faculty members in regions close to their origins.

No item in the listing and description of SCDE faculty characteristics is of itself evidence of parochialism. We realize, for example, a faculty member who attended college only thirty miles from home may have done so in a very cosmopolitan environment. Rather, it is the combination of items—attendance at a nearby college, lack of a tradition of college education within the family, possession of a professional school degree, work in the lower schools, weak enculturation into higher education—that makes campus potency problematic and that suggests parochialism.

All education is potentially broadening, but some educational experiences are more broadening than others. The 75 percent of SCDE faculty in our study who went no further than 300 miles away from home in order to attend college probably attended college in a familiar environment. It may have been urban while the student grew up in a suburban or rural environment yet the urban was a "known" unknown; for example, a young person from rural New Hampshire attending a college in Boston. If there are degrees of culture shock leading to a less parochial view, then the New Hampshire person in Boston is likely to undergo a less threatening experience than that of the Iowa student going to San Francisco.

Most SCDE faculty are first generation college educated. The presence or absence of college degrees and high school completions in one's family history is neither good nor bad; it is merely suggestive of some things and not of some others. For example, given the lack of college backgrounds in the families of future SCDE faculty members, they very likely had little family or home preparation for college. Arguments on behalf of college matriculation may have been made, but there could not have been much experiential conviction for this view in the majority of cases. Chances are good that the arguments came from a belief in education in a general sense, a hope that education or more schooling might lead to a better life, to more income, to higher social status. But there was little likelihood of much advice on how to survive freshman composition, which professors to choose, which dorm to select, or fraternity or sorority to join. Jencks and Riesman (1969) have commented on the differences in students from families where college education is a tradition and from those where it is not.

> In part it is because such families know more about college in general, and are less likely to assume that the nearest is as good as any other. Then, too, low-income students usually work part-time when attending a college, and jobs are often easier to find in one's own home town. The less affluent students are also more likely to attend publicly subsidized institutions that discourage non-locals from applying (p. 167).

There *is* a profound difference between those who attend college following in the footsteps of parents, uncles, aunts, and grandparents and those who attend as representatives of the first generation to do so. Students in the first category have grown up hearing reunion stories, fraternity and sorority talks, Homecoming anecdotes, and the like, while the latter grow up being told that they should think about going to college. They may have heard and participated in discussions in which the types of experience and knowledge acquired through advanced study were necessary. In brief, the first group is acclimated to college even before they arrive. First generation college-goers experience a much different and less helpful rite of passage. Home and family experience teach them little about higher education beyond its desirability.

There is no way of knowing precisely what non-college graduate parents promoted when they urged their future professors of education to continue their schooling. It is, however, unlikely that they did so because of the value of scholarship. It may well be that what little thought they gave to scholarship was unfavorable. College professors were often depicted as educated fools, as impractical people, as individuals who would not know how to "meet a payroll." At the same time negative views of college professors may have been present, there was also likely to be the contradictory view that going to college would provide a passport to a richer life. Thus, a plausible explanation for the lack of interest in sustained inquiry that characterizes some professors of education may be an early lack of experience, knowledge, and sophistication about higher education with long-term implications.

Many professors of education attended low-prestige institutions, more often than not attaining a bachelor's degree in education, followed several years later by a master's in education, and subsequently a doctorate in education. Each of the latter probably was attained while attending school part-time and working full-time in the lower schools. For years the final degree was most often the Ed.D.; recently, it is more likely to be the Ph.D.

Part-time study is unlikely to lead to a full inculcation into the traditions and values of higher education. Many current SCDE faculty undoubtedly worked toward advanced degrees while being employed full-time in the lower schools. The values contrast between higher education and the lower schools is well-known (Lanier, 1986), often described as the ivory tower theorist versus the real world practitioner. Thus, prospective SCDE faculty went through their programs with divided loyalties, a condition that has historically fostered high espousal of lower school affiliation by such individuals upon appointment to higher education faculty.

Thus, our interpretation of the data suggests that professors of education went to low-prestige institutions at which they acquired low-prestige bachelor of science degrees in education. Subsequently, most took jobs as either elementary or secondary school teachers, choices of low social prestige. Still later they studied for and attained second-rate advanced degrees at a variety of institutions. Often, the doctoral degree was acquired at an institution of considerably higher prestige than the one from which the bachelor's degree was acquired. One must add, however, that the degree came from one of the perceived second-rate components of the institution; namely, the college or school of education.

For what purpose do we emphasize the sense of second-rateness in this discussion, and whose second-rateness is it? Most professors would argue for the integrity and value of their advanced degrees. That is not the point. The point is a vast perception exists that the people and their work are second-rate. We conjecture that the sense of second-rateness, perceived or otherwise, plays out in the lives of professors of education in a variety of ways. Having been the object of a perception that either they or their organizations are second-rate for most of their professional lives, some individuals fail to function effectively in the environment in which they work. Perhaps they rationalize and refuse to take the work of higher education seriously, especially sustained research and scholarship. Clark (1987) illustrates how some faculty in other academic units may feel about education faculty:

> Pointing to a fellow professor who until recently had been 'in the inner sanctum of the education establishment that runs [the college]',a professor in the humanities went on to explode about the college of education. '[He] is now a professor in the foundations of education whatever the hell they do over there and that mishmash that goes in all directions, people without disciplines, six characters in search of an author, twelve characters in search of a discipline!' (p. 167).

To be sure, this statement can be heard at almost any institution and in any discipline. It is often uttered by disgruntled faculty nearly totally ignorant of what education faculty do and ill-disposed to learn. Yet one must acknowledge that the view exists. In an earlier chapter, Schwebel notes Judge's observations about the difficulties of living in a professional world seen as faulty by one's ostensible colleagues. The status of a discipline is determined by the degree to which such perceptions are shared by one's colleagues in and out of education, a phenomenon discussed by Burch in a later chapter.

## GENDER AND RACIAL CHARACTERISTICS

Teaching is primarily a female profession; more than 65 percent of all teachers are female. Surveys of the education professoriate consistently find that most teacher educators are men. The education professoriate in our surveys which represents a variety of disciplines within teacher education is approximately 65 percent male, 35 percent female. In 1986 the American Association of Colleges for Teacher Education (AACTE) conducted a study of the secondary education programs of nearly ninety member institutions and found that the faculty was 70 percent male and 30 percent female (American Association of Colleges for Teacher Education, 1987). The 1987 Research About Teacher Education (RATE) survey, which gathered data on faculty teaching the introductory foundations courses, found 72 percent male and 28 percent female. In brief, survey after survey shows the education professoriate to be more than 65 percent male, a condition contrasting sharply with the population of teacher education students which is approximately 70 percent female.

Our data reveal a higher percentage of females in some professional fields, notably elementary and special education. Even in a field such as elementary education, in which over 80 percent of the practitioners are female, only slightly more than half of the faculty are women. Other areas of specialization such as educational administration, higher education, and educational foundations are almost entirely male.

There are also clear differences in gender distribution across professorial ranks. For example, while women account for 30 percent of the secondary education professoriate in the RATE study, they form only 16 percent of the full professor rank. Our study of the professoriate found a similar pattern; 14 percent of the full professors were female and 86 percent male. At the assistant professor level, there was a more even distribution with 46 percent female and 54 percent male. This more balanced representation offers some hope for change for there is a larger pool of women entering the professoriate than previously. In addition, the RATE data indicate that 57 percent of the students in doctoral programs in secondary education are women.

Despite this positive trend, a note of caution must be raised. Other data in our study suggest that women enter the professoriate later, teach more and publish less. These factors could militate against their progress through the tenure and promotion process. For a more balanced gender distribution to be achieved within the education professoriate and its academic ranks, women must continue to complete doctoral programs and be hired at the entry level to the professoriate; they must also progress through the ranks, and the result of this process may not be visible for a number of years.

Minorities are much less represented in the education professoriate than are women. In the RATE study, 2.9 percent of the full professors are minority; 6.4 percent at the associate level; and 9.9 percent at the assistant professor level. The representation of minorities appears to be growing at the lower levels of academic rank, but the growth may be short lived inasmuch as these institutions showed a total of only 8 percent minority in doctoral programs.

The implications of the ethnic imbalances are even more startling. Currently, a conscious intent is found among teacher educators to recruit minority candidates into the teaching profession as well as a rising awareness of the problem (Graham, 1987; Bell & Morsink, 1986). Furthermore, recent predictions, including those by Hodgkinson (1985), argue that by the year 2000, one of every three Americans will be nonwhite. The AACTE data show the gap between the ethnic composition of the education students and the general population demographics. Graham (1987) argues for intensive recruitment of quality minority students for teacher preparation programs. Imig and Imig (1987) observe:

If one accepts the proposition that the work force should reflect the ethnic and racial characteristics of the larger society, then the number of minority teachers is significantly out of line with the society at large. . . . Some suggest that . . . the typical minority youngster could 'meet' only two minority teachers out of the forty teachers whom he or she encounters in twelve years of schooling. Significant interventions to address this problem need to be in the forefront of every policy maker's agenda (p. 53).

Yet, even if the profession were to accomplish the goal of recruiting vastly more minority candidates to teacher preparation programs, another major problem would persist: The near-complete lack of role models both for minority students aspiring to become teachers and for white students needing an understanding of relationships with minority teachers. Teacher education must intensively recruit minority faculty members if the sham of role model absence is to be avoided.

The white male dominance of the faculty of colleges of education remains a relatively undiscussed phenomenon despite the many works dealing with sexism in the academy and the total society. Only recently has a work been devoted to the situation of Black professors in schools of education (Anderson, 1985). While some women and minority faculty members have become department heads and deans, the dominance of white males remains a fundamental characteristic of the professoriate. The implicit and explicit role modeling in this phenomenon is not in keeping with the highest ideals of American society or, indeed, of the composition of the teaching profession.

## LIFE IN THE LOWER SCHOOLS AND ITS IMPLICATIONS

Most current SCDE faculty lived through a variety of prestige levels over a period of years. For those who became secondary school teachers, they generally experienced conflict between the subject matter they were studying, their academic major, and their career choice, teaching. Judge (1982) clearly described some of the attitudes they might have encountered.

> The men and women of arts and sciences make no pretense of loving what they see. Many believe that time spent in a school or college of education is time wasted. Few would have done anything of the sort themselves (for were they not determined to become teachers in *higher* education?) and will not encourage their brighter students in that direction (p. 34).

If they were the brighter students, they endured varying forms of contempt for their career choice from their subject matter professors, possibly even been rebuked for aiming so low in their career choice. If they were not among the brighter, they endured the ignominy of at least suspecting that their subject matter professors thought it all right for *them* to teach school, inasmuch as they were not fit for graduate work in the disciplines.

Once in their teaching careers, however, these same people were suddenly perceived as local experts on biology, literature, history, or mathematics. Schools, like all social organizations, have their pecking orders. The relative prestige of the content one teaches affects one's standing in the school; for example, the English teacher has a higher standing than the driver education teacher. In the ten weeks between college graduation and the first days on the job, an individual can go from being a low-ranking teacher education student at the university to being a teacher of American history in the school setting.

When such individuals went on for graduate study, they inevitably found their potential defined or limited by what was available for full-time teachers; namely, part-time study with the faculty of the nearest SCDE. Those with skill, perseverance, luck, or time ultimately would complete a doctorate and, in years past, assume a position in higher education alongside "real" professors. Generally, their salaries, office amenities, and other matters would teach them the priorities of higher education. In many cases, the result would often not be an aggressive, confident faculty member.

In his at times whimsical *American Graduate Schools of Education*, Judge (1982) presents a scenario that may have been the pattern for many current professors of education:

> As part of his course work over the last two years, the student, in his senior year, completed several weeks of student teaching (practice teaching) in local schools. His work was supervised by a coordinator designated by the university and recognized as an effective teacher of English language and literature. . . . His coordinator cares about him but doesn't work for nothing. The coordinator's reward is a number of tuition units which he cashes in on campus as a substantial contribution to his course. He is well on his way towards his doctorate in, of course, the Graduate School of Education and hopes one day soon to become a director of curriculum at a good suburban school (p. 23).

Except for the fact that Judge projects his teacher coordinator desiring to be a curriculum director, he has encapsulated pieces of the careers of many professors of education. In years past, the individual might have gone on to a position at a college or university.

There is a compelling irony in Judge's vignette. The teacher in question is recognized as expert in the high school in which he teachers. He is one of the leaders of the English department, the bastion in the high school to promote culture and retard the growth of barbarism. The irony in his reward for such exemplary behavior is the right to seek a degree from the portion of higher education considered by culture leaders to be the center of barbarism on the campus; namely, the school or college of education.

In an earlier article (Ducharme & Agne, 1982), we referred to the extensive lower school experience of SCDE faculty in a laudatory way because of its importance to the irrelevance argument often made about SCDE faculty work.

> Our study reveals that the matter of SCDE faculty experience in public and private lower schooling is one on which there should be no future doubt. The present cadre of SCDE faculty is anything but inexperienced in the public schools. Our survey reveals overwhelmingly that most SCDE faculty had extensive experience in the schools prior to their appointments in higher education. Seventy-one percent of those surveyed had appointments in the lower schools, of that group, 87 percent had three or more years; 57 percent more than five; and 31 percent more than nine. The experiences were in a variety of specific roles; classroom teacher (65 percent), counselor (8 percent). department chair (14 percent, and administrator (14 percent). Some individuals filled more than one role during their time in the schools (p. 32).

Useful as these backgrounds may be for teacher educators, they *may* be counterproductive to their enculturation to the higher education environment.

The considerable experience that professors of education have had in the lower schools is, for many, the major enculturating experience of their lives. Our interviews with faculty suggest that the years in the public schools were times of success and accomplishment. Life in the lower schools is marked by much activity, great busyness, rapid decision-making, and quick responses. While not necessarily anti-intellectual, the life is not often one of inquiry and introspection. In *A Place Called School*, Goodlad (1984) demonstrates the levels of conformity and consistency throughout schooling, the good and the bad.

> In this connection, one disappointing implication of the data is that the schools enjoying the most favorable perceptions appear not to have taken advantage of this asset in creating such classroom procedures. For them, too, certain conventional ways of conducting the schooling enterprises are the preferred norm. The principal and teachers in these schools, who in general

perceived themselves to have a great deal of power and influence, did not take advantage of these attributes to redesign teaching and learning. Conversely, the teachers with more negative views of their workplace were no more likely to demonstrate markedly inferior pedagogy. Both groups, it appears, were conditioned and restrained by the power of existing regularities. They did not attempt to explore other possibilities (p. 249).

In Goodlad's view, individuals generally behave similarly in school environments regardless of stronger or weaker characteristics. This view makes a powerful statement about the impact of an institution on individual behaviors.

We argue that many of the behaviors and beliefs implicit in Goodlad's comments, and in other contemporary descriptions of schooling, are inappropriate for a potent professorial life in an SCDE. They suggest a sameness; a once-demonstrated, never-questioned attitude; and little aptitude for inquiry. We are not arguing that the behaviors are the right ones or the wrong for lower education; nor was Goodlad. But they appear to be pervasive and adequate to get one through the day in the lower schools. Carried over to a career in higher education, they are a parody of the academic life.

## MEAGER FUNDS AND RESPECT

The meager funding of SCDEs has long been an issue. The condition has prevailed despite years during which education programs contributed mightily to institutional budgets. Peseau (1982) observes the way constant underfunding may create an attitude of acceptance of lower support on the part of SCDEs; "We limit what we do to the bare essentials, retreat to the most secure and defensive position, and discourage differences. Worse—far worse and more tragic—*we come to accept starvation and poverty as a normal condition.*" (p. 15) We wonder about the infrequency of confrontation over the low support accorded professional education preparation programs. SCDE faculty have rarely made their own fiscal support a major issue; the National Education Association (NEA) and the American Federation of Teachers, (AFT) while occasionally calling for the improvement of professional preparation programs, have rarely made the funding of such programs an issue. We contend that there is a relationship between the social class origins and the perceived second-rate status of SCDE faculty and the infrequency and ineptness of moves toward additional support. Again, Judge (1982) makes an apt comment:

> It seems unfortunate that the canard 'schools of education are at the bottom of the pile and deserve to be' should be repeated so often with no serious attempt to discover precisely what the canard means. It is no great fun to work in places that are constantly sniffed at or spat upon (p. 25).

Indeed, life in an organization perceived as having little status or importance is "no great fun."

> Unfortunately, the low self-esteem of teacher educators for their own work is an outgrowth of the inferior status which American higher education has long assigned to the preparation of teachers. Some teacher educators who question the importance of their own field begin to seek ways to achieve conventional academic status (Howsam, Corrigan, Denemark, & Nash, 1976, p. 108).

In the more than ten years since that statement, conditions have apparently changed very little: "Data from a major state university show that twice as much money is spent on educating an engineer as a teacher and almost 60 percent more on educating a business graduate" (National Commission for Excellence in Teacher Education, 1985, p. 22).

There is no indication anywhere that, except for occasional grants that augment available funds, conditions are any different for these professors of education involved in the preparation of other educational professionals such as administrators and counselors. In fact, in many institutions, these programs are, in part, carried by revenues generated by undergraduate teacher education.

A tantalizing aspect of the financial support issue is that, historically, SCDEs have generated much tuition income for other portions of the institutions, income rarely returned proportionately to the SCDEs. Indeed, the condition must still prevail as new programs continue to emerge. Recent surveys indicate that more than 1,200 institutions have teacher preparation programs, an increase of 100 since the early 1970s (National Commission for Excellence in Teacher Education, 1985, p. 17). Institutional altruism is a doubtful source for the emergence of such programs. The quick births and demises of

Master of Arts in Teaching (MAT) programs, occurrences finely tuned to available funds, suggest that any altruistic missions served by SCDEs are not the result of institutional purpose.

The lack of equal funding for education programs is not the cause of the condition and reputation of SCDEs on campuses. Rather, it may be the other way around. SCDE faculty may be at times the unwilling cause of some of their own problems. The manner and the quality of how the education professoriate is inducted and initiated into higher education may be a contributor. Certainly the issue is compelling and needs further exploration and study.

Funding is a reflection of the value placed on the activity. Low funding within an organization for one of its parts reflects lack of value. It is difficult to be a potent member of a society or organization in which one's membership or right of participation is questioned. Difficulty is further exacerbated if the "product" one develops or the work one does has low esteem. Some have seen the work of SCDE faculty as unimportant to society. We earlier contended that (Ducharme & Agne, 1982):

> SCDE faculty either do no true research or they do research of little merit; they are not scholarly enough, and not university-focused. . . . The general public sees SCDE faculty as those who provide preparation for jobs that do not exist, those responsible for what some see as the deplorable state of the public schools (p. 31).

Schwebel (1985) talks about low esteem for what faculty do: "The EF's [education faculty] mission—to educate the nonelite of the nation—does not rank high among social priorities, as these are defined by the dynamics of the economic-political system" (p. 4).

The apparent incongruity between a society that appears to value education as much as American society does and the low esteem held for educating the nonelites in the society is somewhat explained by Judge (1982) in his comment on America's values regarding education.

> Moreover, it may be a misleading oversimplification to argue that Americans place a particularly high value on 'education' in some broad and unspecific sense, starting from induction into a liberal, humane culture. Many Americans have themselves commented on the national tendency to value education for what it

can deliver, for the credentials it can furnish, for the gates to prosperity and status it opens (p. 30).

And, as Schwebel (1985) points out, the "induction into a liberal, humane culture" is generally done in "quality education in private and upper-middle-class suburban schools to reproduce its leadership in business, government, and the professions, and its knowledge producers" (p. 4).

SCDE faculty instruct teacher education students who occasionally report that their peers in other academic units demean them and their curriculum. Students may become defensive, wondering why they and their chosen field are poorly regarded. As a consequence, they may question the efficacy of their SCDE faculty who might otherwise be seen as competent and caring professors. All too often, the students themselves present problems to SCDE faculty:

> Teacher educators encounter many learners that are not easily engaged in serious intellectual growth with the aim of improving schools and professional practice. Not only are the academic interests and abilities of the student majority low when compared with the college educated population as a whole, but the learners affective propensities are equally problematic (Lanier, 1986, p. 542).

While Lanier is talking about teacher education students, one can assume similarities among nearly all SCDE student groups in that a teacher education background is a common experience for future graduate students in administration, counseling, and other education-related graduate areas.

The low social status origins, early family and community values, lower school teaching experience, marginal institutional affiliation during doctoral studies, and only occasional forays into academic activities may all contribute to SCDE faculty being less concerned with the traditional research and scholarship emphases of higher education and more attuned to the pragmatic matters of the schools.

SCDE faculty and their students present a case of like teaching like; both groups share backgrounds, values, and norms. The chief distinction between the two may be the doctorate and the higher status of the professor. For in-service students, these distinctions are often not viewed as formidable inasmuch as they have either seen or know of people in their current status who have acquired the doctorate and subsequent higher education faculty status.

All of the above has led to a confusion about roles for professors of education in colleges and universities. On many campuses, faculty fill three metaphorical roles: beasts of burden, facilitators, and academicians. In the first are those who flit from place to place, carrying equipment, reprints, games, and transparencies as they do differing versions of academic dog- and-pony shows; the second, those largely "contentless" persons who apparently see their function in life as bridging the work of others; and the third, those who teach, advise, study, and write with inquiry, rigor, and scholarship uppermost (Ducharme & Agne, 1987).

## CONCLUSION

This chapter may be depressing in its seemingly deterministic views, including its bald statements of the lack of status of some of the work of SCDE faculty and of the questionable nature of some SCDE faculty and students. It need not be so. The study of the education professoriate is a necessary if somewhat painful activity. SCDE faculty must first know and understand themselves and their values, aspirations, strengths, and weaknesses. This chapter provides some of that information. Only through the possession of knowledge can the education professoriate participate in deliberations about its future.

The future for the professoriate is clouded. For generations many SCDE faculty have spent their careers in providing preparation, theory, and support for legions of undergraduate teacher education students. Change clearly is in the air, as Schwebel's discussion underscores. There is simply too much demand for change from too many sources for conditions to remain as they are. The combination of pressures from the Holmes group and several state reports for a fifth year of preparation is sufficiently great that some institutions have moved from traditional undergraduate preparation to a fifth year. Such a move has considerable implications for SCDE faculty. This is but one area in which change is likely.

The future may also be different with respect to SCDE faculty and the traditional values of the academy. New appointees to faculty positions are much more research-oriented then has been the case in the past. Currently little in the way of hard data is found to support this contention, but the writers have experienced this in their own hirings and have encountered the same viewpoint in conversations with deans, chairs, and directors. For example, the three most recently appointed faculty—each a woman with one-or two-year-old

Ph.D.s—at the University of Vermont had a combined total of seven refereed publications, all prior to their initial appointments as tenure-line, assistant professors. This stands in sharp contrast to what was common a decade ago. Other contributors to this volume report similar trends. Each appointee has begun her career at the University of Vermont with a research line in mind upon appointment. Both the specific experience and the implicit attitude suggest a changing portrait of the SCDE faculty over the next decade, a portrait perhaps more in accord with traditional academic norms.

Schwebel (1985) has observed this phenomenon:

> Difficult though it is to document, there is reason to believe that the quality of educational research is improving with the development of the AERA, the increased research sophistication of each new cohort of doctorates in education, the reduced enrollments in education, and the academic press for publication (p. 4).

The predicted change will also present new problems and questions. While such faculty may be more attuned to higher education norms, will they be effective with lower school faculties? Will their research and scholarship be both academically respectable and utilitarian? How will new faculty with different expectations blend in with the older faculty? These and other questions will accompany any changes. These are encouraging questions. Certainly, it is better to ask if there is a "fit" between faculty research and scholarship and the schools than it is to ask if there is any faculty research and scholarship.

Whatever the directions of the future, SCDE faculty must be prepared for a viable role. The likelihood of their playing that role will be greatly enhanced by the degree to which they become potent forces on their campuses. They must overcome the weak vestiges of their past and enhance their strengths. They must contribute to a future that puts to rest both warranted and unwarranted stereotypes.

## REFERENCES

American Association of Colleges for Teacher Education. (1987). *Teaching and teachers: Facts and figures.* Washington, D.C.: American Association of Colleges for Teacher Education.

Anderson, J. (1984). *Toward a history and bibliography of the Afro-American doctorate and professoriate in education, 1986 to 1980: The Black education professoriate.* Minneapolis: Society of Professors of Education, College of Education, University of Minnesota.

Bell, M., & Morsink, C. (1986). Quality and equity in the preparation of black teachers. *Journal of Teacher Education, 37* (2), 10–15.

Clark, B. R. (1987). *The academic life: Small worlds, different worlds.* Princeton, N.J.: The Carnegie Foundation for the Advancement of Teaching.

Ducharme, E., & Agne, R. (1982). The education professoriate: A research-based perspective. *Journal of Teacher Education, 33* (6), 30–36.

_____ (1987). Professors of education: Beasts of burden, facilitators, or academicians. *Journal of Human Behavior and Learning, 4* (2), 1–8.

Fuller, F., & Bown, O. (1975). Becoming a teacher. In K. Ryan (Ed.), *Teacher education* (74th Yearbook of the National Society for the Study of Education, Pt. 2) pp. 25–52. Chicago: University of Chicago Press.

Goodlad, J. (1984). *A place called school.* New York: McGraw-Hill Book Company.

Graham, P. (1987). Black teachers: A drastically scarce resource. *Phi Delta Kappan, 68* (8), 598–605.

Howsam, R., Corrigan, D., Denemark, G., & Nash, R. (1976). *Educating a profession.* Washington, D.C.: American Association of Colleges for Teacher Education.

Hodgkinson, H. (1987). *All one system.* Washington, D.C.: Institute for Educational Leadership, Inc.

Imig, D. G., & Imig, D. R. (1987). Strengthening and maintaining the pool of qualified teachers. In C. Magrath & R. Egbert (Eds.), *Strengthening teacher education: The challenges to college and university leaders.* San Francisco: Jossey-Bass Publishers.

Jencks, C., & Riesman, D. (1969). *The academic revolution.* New York: Doubleday.

Judge, H. (1982). *American graduate schools of education: A view from abroad.* New York: Ford Foundation Report.

Lanier, J. (1986). Research on teacher education. In M. C. Wittrock (Ed.), *Handbook of Research on Teaching*, (3rd ed.). New York: Macmillan Publishing Company.

Lortie, D. C. (1975). *Schoolteacher: A sociological study.* Chicago: University of Chicago Press.

National Commission for Excellence in Teacher Education. (1985). *A call for change in teacher education.* Washington D.C.: American Association of Colleges for Teacher Education.

Peseau, B. A. (1982). Developing an adequate resource base for teacher education. *Journal of Teacher Education, 33* (4), 13–15.

Raths, J. (1985). *A profile of methods instructors in teacher education.* Washington D.C.: American Association of Colleges for Teacher Education. (ERIC Document Reproduction Service No. SPO26 O37.)

Schwebel, M. (1985). The clash of cultures in academe: The university and the education faculty. *Journal of Teacher Education, 36* (4), 2–7.

# 6

# Perceptions of the Role and Scholarly Reputation of the Education Professoriate

## BARBARA G. BURCH

### INTRODUCTION

Faculty in schools, colleges, and departments of education (SCDEs) have traditionally attempted to respond to expectations of school practitioners as well as those of the university community. The demands on the education professor today are greater and more diverse than ever before and, in many instances, conflicting. Colleges and universities require increased research and publication activity; teachers and other school practitioners want immediately useful help in meeting classroom demands; state officials demand assistance in developing and implementing various state mandates. As a result, considerable concern has arisen about the work of education professors.

As is stressed throughout this volume, SCDE professors are members of a community of scholars who value intellectual achievement and the requirements of scholarship. There are many legitimate forms of intellectual achievement, but the university, according to Bok (1987),

> . . . attaches special value to inquiry that is abstract, theoretical, or interesting for its own sake. They [scholars] typically assign a lesser status to matters that have immediate, practical utility. . . . [Thus,] from these beliefs . . . comes a tendency to value research, and while teaching 'may call for ingenuity of the highest token, . . . [it is] rarely the stuff of which academic reputations are made' (pp. 76–77).

Academic reputations are rarely made as a result of good teaching or professional service. Thus, SCDE professors face a serious dilemma: They must exemplify good teaching and provide practical and useful professional service in an academic world that values scholarship more than teaching and service combined. If SCDE professors are to be held in high regard in the higher education community, they must be esteemed as scholars as well as respected preparers of practitioners.

Several factors complicate SCDE faculty role expectations and affect their reputational status. Education faculty joined the university in substantial numbers beginning in the 1920s with the responsibility to produce vast numbers of trained teachers, as Schwebel discussed earlier. Although the demand for producing large numbers of teachers has declined, long years of mass-producing teachers for a growing population established a preeminent role definition for SCDE professors. SCDE professors also produce more master's and doctoral graduates than are typically produced in other fields; as a result, they have higher graduate faculty-student ratios and higher advising loads than faculty in other departments. SCDE faculty devote at least as much time as faculty in other disciplines to instruction and preparation, often teaching courses requiring supervision of field and clinical experiences. Additionally, SCDE professors spend more time in service-related functions than do non-SCDE faculty.

Other factors affecting the reputational status of the education professoriate include low fiscal support, an uninformed belief that education students are less than first-rate academically, and lack of a clear definition of the academic field of education [cf. Lanier (1984) and Ducharme (1985)]. While these factors were not included in the study reported herein, readers should keep them in mind inasmuch as they help shape perceptions about education faculty.

Professorial responsibilities in teaching, research, and service are discussed with increasing frequency. Questions focus on the necessity for all SCDE professors to achieve in all three areas, and debate is rife. Must every education professor be a researcher? Must all education professors publish in order to enjoy the fruits of the rewards system? Should scholarly activity in a professional school take a different form from that in other academic fields of inquiry?

These questions and related issues are discussed throughout this volume; they are fundamental to understanding the education professoriate. Partial answers are provided by a survey of SCDE professors and non-SCDE professors that was suggested by the dialogues that led to this volume. The survey was conducted in an effort to answer two vexing questions: What are the views of education professors about their roles and their reputational status, and how do professors outside of education perceive the role and reputation of professors of education?

## THE STUDY

The study was undertaken to obtain preliminary insights into the beliefs and commitments SCDE professors have toward scholarly activities. Examining the perceptions of SCDE professors in comparison to non-SCDE professorial colleagues is one approach to understanding SCDE professional roles and reputations. While the study focuses on perceptions related to research and scholarship, considerable overlap and interplay exist among teaching, research, and service. Hence, questions about teaching and service activities were also included on the questionnaire mailed to participants.

The findings provide self-reported information and viewpoints from a limited sample of faculty in education and other disciplines. It is perhaps an illustration of what professors can do to develop further the knowledge base about the education professoriate, namely, conduct studies of limited scope to illuminate diffuse questions. This study reports the reflections of education professors about themselves as well as the perceptions of professors from other disciplines about them, and it complements earlier work by Schwebel (1982) as well as that reported by Ducharme and Agne in this volume.

Information was collected in 1985 from selected SCDE professors involved in teacher education, both from an administrative and teaching perspective, all of whom were professing at least some portion of their time. Deans who were full-time administrators were not included. The SCDE professors were drawn from a random sample of institutional representatives from the American Association of Colleges for Teacher Education (AACTE) membership roster. The non-SCDE professors were a random sample of professor/department heads in arts and sciences disciplines drawn from the *Yearbook of Higher Education* (1982–83) from both large and small public and private institutions. The researcher explored the following questions:

1. What are the primary reasons that individuals choose to become SCDE professors, and how satisfied are they with their choices?
2. How do SCDE professors define scholarly activity?
3. What is the nature of the scholarly activity of SCDE professors?
4. What are the perceptions relative to teaching, scholarly activity, and service of SCDE professors?
5. What are the prevailing perceptions of the role expectations and status of SCDE professors?

The data do not allow for comparisons between SCDE and non-SCDE professors on every point, especially with regard to the first question. Conjectures can be made, however, on the relationships among variables as well as on the patterns of role expectations for SCDE professors.

## METHODOLOGY

A questionnaire was mailed to 180 SCDE and non-SCDE professors. One hundred three professors (57 percent) responded, of which sixty were SCDE professors (58 percent) and forty-three (42 percent) non-SCDE professors. The latter represented fields such as communications, business, engineering, natural sciences, social sciences, fine arts, and other liberal arts areas. Demographic information was obtained concerning the type and size of institutions represented, rank and teaching experience of the professors, and some indication of what influenced them to pursue the professoriate as a career. Questions were also included to determine definitions of scholarly activity; the extent to which professors are engaged in such activity; assessments of SCDE professors of themselves and by non-SCDE professors in relation to expected professorial roles; and expectations and views about scholarly activity and their work as professors.

*Population*

Sixty-eight percent of SCDE respondents and 65 percent of non-SCDE respondents were full professors. Seventeen percent of SCDE respondents held associate rank and 15 percent assistant rank. Thirty-three percent of the SCDE professors defined their assignments as primarily administrative rather than teaching. This rather high figure reflects the many program areas in a typical school of education for which professors have some administrative responsibility. Ninety-five percent of the SCDE professors and 30 percent of the non-SCDE professors had prior K–12 teaching experience with an average of seven years experience for SCDE professors and fewer than two years for non-SCDE professors. SCDE professors from public higher education institutions had slightly more K–12 experience than their counterparts in private institutions.

*Institutions*

Twenty-five percent of the private institutions had enrollments of fewer than one thousand. Sixty-four percent of the public institutions and 19 percent of the private institutions represented by the SCDE professor group had enrollments of 10,000 or more. Seventy-five percent of the public higher education institutions represented by the SCDE professor group offered graduate degrees; 41 percent of the private schools offered graduate degrees.

## REASONS INDIVIDUALS CHOSE TO BECOME SCDE PROFESSORS AND THE LEVEL OF SATISFACTION WITH THEIR CHOICES

SCDE professors decide to work in higher education for essentially the same reasons as do non-SCDE professors. The most frequent reasons given were a desire to make a difference, enjoyment of teaching, intellectual stimulation, the lifestyle of a college professor, and the encouragement of and influence over others. Other reasons included the status and prestige of the profession, economic considerations, and limited choices because of other circumstances. Only *one* of the 103 professors indicated an "opportunity to do research" as a primary reason for becoming a professor.

Seventy-nine percent of the professors studied were in the first generation in their families to work in higher education. SCDE professors from public institutions were slightly less content with their careers than private institution counterparts; however, 82 percent of the SCDE professors would again choose the education professoriate as a career. Those who would no longer select the education professoriate gave varying reasons including low status, desire to be more highly valued, and a preference for doing something different.

## DEFINITIONS OF SCHOLARLY ACTIVITY

The diverse interpretations of the term scholarly activity by professors complicated a clear definition. Respondents were asked to give one or more descriptors of scholarly activity, hence, percentages exceed 100. The most frequently cited descriptors given by SCDE and non-SCDE professors are in Table I. (In all the tables, the N for SCDE professors is 60 and the N for non-SCDE professors is 43.)

**Table I**
Descriptors of Scholarly Activity

| Descriptor | SCDE Professors Percent | Non-SCDE Professors Percent |
|---|---|---|
| Research | 90% | 58% |
| Writing | 51% | 52% |
| Reading | 24% | 7% |
| Attending Professional Meetings | 31% | 39% |

Research and writing were the most frequent descriptors for scholarly activity by both SCDE and non-SCDE professors. Other descriptors were pursuit of knowledge, attending professional meetings, participating in intellectual discussions, teaching, consulting, curriculum development, committee work, dialogue with other scholars, political activities, service to client groups, and advising students.

Most of the definitions of scholarly activity described processes rather than observable outcomes. For example: generate, translate, and apply new knowledge for client use; engage in activity that improves instruction; systematic inquiry that adds knowledge and promotes improvement in education; share professional information, concepts, and ideas; write, research, and publish; engage in activities that affect educational change; investigate problems and issues related to major field; read in the field; express oneself in creative and new knowledge- producing ways; and engage in activities that involve discerning, assembling, organizing, and/or teaching of information to others.

More importantly, 32 percent of the SCDE professors, most of whom had primary roles in teaching rather than administration, thought scholarly activity should be defined differently for SCDE professors than for non-SCDE professors. These professors would like to see more value given to professional service activities as a scholarly endeavor.

## NATURE OF SCHOLARLY ACTIVITY

In addition to determining whether SCDE professors are currently engaged in research, the researcher considered participation in other activities. These activities included opportunity for scholarly dialogue, publication, major presentations, professional service, and professional reading.

Seventy-six percent of the SCDE professors were currently engaged in research activity, the same proportion as non-SCDE professors. The average amount of time spent in research by SCDE professors was 12 percent. Slightly more research activity was undertaken among SCDE professors in public institutions than in private institutions. Almost all professors thought that they had considerable opportunity to control their own time; however, opportunity for controlling one's own time was considerably greater among SCDE professors whose primary responsibility was teaching rather than administrative. This is an interesting finding in conjunction with Gideonse's discussion in a later chapter.

### Opportunity for Scholarly Dialogue

The opportunity to engage in intellectually stimulating scholarly dialogue varied considerably. Eighteen percent indicated that they had "very little" opportunity for such dialogue, while 39 percent indicated they had "considerable opportunity." SCDE professors in private colleges had slightly more opportunity for intellectually stimulating dialogue than did their counterparts in public institutions; SCDE professors with administrative responsibilities had more opportunity than those with only teaching responsibilities. Virtually no difference was found in the amount of opportunity for scholarly dialogue that existed among SCDE professors and their colleagues outside of education.

## Frequency of Publication

Frequency of publication over the past five years included books as well as articles in scholarly journals, as shown in Table II. Twenty-four percent of SCDE professors and 23 percent of non-SCDE professors had no journal publications in the past five years; 75 percent had no books published during that same time period. Ten percent of the SCDE professors had published twenty or more articles in scholarly journals during the past five years; only 2 percent of the non-SCDE professors published at this level. These findings are similar to those reported by Ducharme and Agne (1982). There was no difference in publication frequency among SCDE professors relative to whether their roles were primarily administrative or teaching.

**Table II**
Publications for Five Years

| | Journal Articles | | | | Books | | Book Chapters | | | |
|---|---|---|---|---|---|---|---|---|---|---|
| Professors | None | 1–5 | 6–19 | 20+ | Yes | No | None | 1–5 | 6–19 | 20+ |
| SCDE | 24% | 46% | 18% | 10% | 25% | 75% | 48% | 46% | 3% | 2% |
| Non-SCDE | 23% | 54% | 21% | 2% | 23% | 72%* | 58% | 30% | 5% | 0% |

*Total less than 100 percent due to nonresponses.

## Major Presentations

Major presentations in the last five years are indicated in Table III. Twenty-seven percent of the SCDE and 10 percent of the non-SCDE professors had given twenty or more major presentations. When the data were sorted contrasting public and private institutions, all SCDE professors from public higher education institutions had given major presentations during the past five years, while 21 percent of the private institution SCDE professors had made no major presentations during the past five years.

**Table III**
Major Presentations for Past Five Years

| Professors | None | 1–5 | 6–19 | 20+ |
|---|---|---|---|---|
| SCDE | 3% | 38% | 32% | 27% |
| Non-SCDE | 7% | 65% | 18% | 10% |

## Professional Service

As shown in Table IV, both SCDE and non-SCDE professors provided professional service activities during the past five years, although considerable difference was found in the frequency of these activities. While 85 percent of the SCDE professors had provided six or more professional service activities in the past five years, only about 35 percent of the non-SCDE professors had been similarly engaged. All professors in public institutions had provided some service activity in the past five years; in the private institutions 31 percent of the non-SCDE professors had provided no service activities during the last five years. Both SCDE and non-SCDE professors in public higher education institutions provided considerably more service activities than their counterparts in private institutions.

**Table IV**
Professors' Service Activities for Past Five Years

| Professor | None | 1–5 | 6–19 | 20+ |
|---|---|---|---|---|
| SCDE | 0% | 13% | 23% | 62%* |
| Non-SCDE | 7% | 51% | 26% | 9% |

*Total less than 100 percent due to professors not responding.

*Professional Readings*

The two journals most frequently read by more than one-half of the SCDE professors were the *Phi Delta Kappan* and *Educational Leadership*. The third most frequently cited journal, read by 26 percent of the SCDE professors, was the *Journal of Teacher Education;* 10 percent of the SCDE professors named the *AERA Journal* and the *Chronicle of Higher Education*. The most frequently cited book recently read by SCDE professors was *In Search of Excellence*. The readings of Non-SCDE professors represented a wide variety of specialties and fields. The only book listed as read by both SCDE and non-SCDE professors was *Megatrends*. Unfortunately, the data available cannot be used to support or challenge Gideonse's (Chapter 7) data regarding the small amount of SCDE professorial time devoted to professional reading.

TEACHING, SCHOLARLY, AND SERVICE REPUTATIONS

Perceptions of SCDE professors and non-SCDE professors were explored relative to the intellectual power, teaching ability, scholarly activity, and service activities of SCDE professors.

*Intellectual Power*

Table V presents professors' perceptions of the intellectual power of SCDE professors as compared to professors in non-SCDE fields. Table VI summarizes professors' views of their own intellectual powers as compared to others in their disciplines.

**Table V**
Perceptions of Intellectual Power of SCDE Professors
Compared to Professors in Non-SCDE Fields

| Intellectual Power of Education Profs. | View of SCDE Profs. | View of Non-SCDE Profs. |
| --- | --- | --- |
| Less than others | 21% | 35% |
| Same as others | 77% | 63% |
| Greater than others | 2% | 2% |

**Table VI**
Professors' Perceptions of Their Own Intellectual Power
Compared with Other Professors in Same Disciplines

| Intellectual Power | SCDE Profs. | Non-SCDE Profs. |
| --- | --- | --- |
| Less than others | 0% | 5% |
| Same as others | 66% | 67% |
| Greater than others | 34% | 28% |

Twenty-one percent of the SCDE professors indicated that SCDE professors had less intellectual power than non-SCDE professors; 35 percent of the non-SCDE professors held this perception. None of the SCDE professors saw themselves as having less intellectual power than other SCDE professors, while 5 percent of the non-SCDE professors saw themselves with less intellectual power than their colleagues. A considerable number of both SCDE and non-SCDE professors felt that they personally had greater intellectual power than most of their colleagues.

## Teaching Ability

Table VII presents perceptions of the SCDE professor's teaching ability as viewed by SCDE and non-SCDE professors, and professors' perceptions of their own teaching ability when compared to other professors in their disciplines.

The majority of SCDE professors believed that SCDE professors are better teachers than their non-SCDE colleagues. This view is not widely shared by non-SCDE professors. The majority of all the professors felt their own teaching ability was greater than that of other

**Table VII**
Perceptions of Teaching Ability

| | Teaching Ability of SCDE Professors as Viewed by SCDE and Non-SCDE Professors | | Professors Own Teaching Ability Compared to Other Professors in Same Discipline | |
| | View of SCDE Prof. | View of Non-SCDE Prof. | View of SCDE Prof. | View of Non-SCDE Prof. |
|---|---|---|---|---|
| Less than others | 2% | 18% | 0% | 0% |
| Same as others | 19% | 70% | 34% | 32% |
| Greater than others | 79% | 12% | 66% | 68% |

professors in their disciplines. None of the responding professors saw themselves as having less teaching ability than any other professors, although a few saw SCDE professors having less teaching ability than other professors.

*Scholarly Activity*

Perceptions of scholarly activity are presented in Tables VIII and IX. A much larger percentage of both SCDE and non-SCDE professors viewed SCDE professors as having less scholarly productivity than non-SCDE professors. Twenty-four percent of all the professors viewed themselves as less productive than other professors in their own disciplines. Only a small percentage of SCDE and non-SCDE professors thought that SCDE professors had greater scholarly productivity than other professors. Thirty-four percent of the SCDE and 17 percent of the non-SCDE professors felt that they had greater scholarly productivity than others in their own professorial groups. These perceptions appear to support Ducharme and Agne's (Chapter V) assessment of scholarly productivity within the academy.

Professors were also asked to indicate their perceptions of the scholarly productivity of SCDE professors as a group as well as the productivity of SCDE professors in their own institutions. These perceptions are presented in TABLE X.

Sixty-two percent of the SCDE professors felt that the scholarly productivity of SCDE professors was less than adequate. However, only 46 percent of the SCDE professors perceived the scholarly productivity of SCDE professors as less than adequate in their own institutions. Three percent of the SCDE professors believed that SCDE professors were more than adequate in scholarly productivity;

**Table VIII**

Perceptions of Scholarly Activity of SCDE
Professors as Viewed by SCDE and Non-SCDE Professors

| Education Professor's Scholarly Activity | View of SCDE Professors | View of Non-SCDE Professors |
|---|---|---|
| Less than non-SCDE professors | 43% | 43% |
| Same as non-SCDE professors | 50% | 54% |
| Greater than non-SCDE professors | 7% | 3% |

however, 32 percent of the SCDE professors thought the scholarly productivity of SCDE professors in their own institutions was more adequate. The private college SCDE professors perceived the scholarly productivity of SCDE professors in their own institutions at a higher level of adequacy than did the public college professors.

**Table IX**

Professors' Perceptions of Their Own Scholarly Activity
Compared with Other Professors in the Same Discipline

| Scholarly Productivity | View of SCDE Professors | View of Non-SCDE Professors |
|---|---|---|
| Less than others | 24% | 22% |
| Same as others | 42% | 61% |
| Greater than others | 34% | 17% |

**Table X**

Perceptions of Scholarly Productivity of Education
Professors as Viewed by Education Professors

| Extent of Scholarly Productivity | For all SCDE Professors Nationally | Professors in Own Institution |
|---|---|---|
| More than adequate | 3% | 32% |
| Adequate | 35% | 22% |
| Less than adequate | 62% | 46% |

*Service Activity*

Table XI presents the service activity of SCDE professors compared to non-SCDE professors. Ninety percent of the SCDE professors believed that their service activities were greater than that of other professors. Fifty-nine percent of the SCDE professors thought their own service activity was greater than that of non-SCDE professorial colleagues. The extent to which SCDE professors saw themselves as being more productive than other professors in providing service activities was considerably greater in public institutions than in private.

**Table XI**
Perceptions of Service Activity of Education Professors
Compared to Noneducation Professors

| Extent of Service Activity | Education Professors' View of Education Professors | Education Professors' View of Self |
|---|---|---|
| Less than others | — | 4% |
| Same as others | 10% | 37% |
| Greater than others | 90% | 59% |

## PERCEPTIONS OF ROLE AND STATUS OF SCDE PROFESSORS

Fifty percent of the SCDE professors believed that the university's role expectation *is* different for SCDE professors, although only 35 percent of the non-SCDE professors agreed with this view. Fifty-four percent of the SCDE professors believed that the role expectation *should* be different; only 14 percent of the non-SCDE professors agreed. More SCDE professors with primarily administrative roles felt that the role expectations for SCDE professors should be different than did SCDE professors whose primary role was teaching.

The most often cited difference in role expectation which SCDE professors perceived as existing and believed *should* exist was an acknowledgement of "the considerable amount of contact time spent in field work and relating to the world of practice in the K–12 schools." Other perceived differences reported by SCDE professors were that they were expected to carry a greater work load and to be better teachers. They also felt less valued and recognized for their contributions to the institution than non-SCDE colleagues.

### Scholarly Activity

Asked to comment on expectations for scholarly activity within their institutions, 68 percent of the SCDE professors and 47 percent of the non-SCDE professors felt that their institutions' expectation for scholarly activity was high. All non-SCDE professors felt there was at least some expectation. Scholarly activity expectations were somewhat higher in public institutions than in private.

## Quality of Teaching

Seventeen percent of all of the professors felt that the SCDE professor's quality of teaching was less valued than that of other professors in the university. Nineteen percent of the SCDE professors felt that their quality of teaching was more valued than that of other professors, while only 3 percent of the non-SCDE professors agreed with this perception. Seventy-nine percent of all the professors, SCDE and non-SCDE, in both public and private institutions felt that there was no difference as to the way quality of teaching was valued in their institutions.

## Research and Publication

Sixty-one percent of the SCDE professors and 34 percent of the non-SCDE professors believed that SCDE professors were less valued for their research and publication than other professors. None of the non-SCDE professors felt that their SCDE colleagues were more valued than they, and 2 percent of the SCDE professors believed their publications and research were more valued than that of other colleagues on campus. The individuals who constituted the 2 percent were private school administrators.

Eighty-four percent of the SCDE professors and 91 percent of the non-SCDE professors agreed that involvement in research had a positive effect on teaching. Sixty-seven percent of the SCDE professors believed that professors should be expected to publish at least annually. Fifteen percent of the SCDE professors and 10 percent of the non-SCDE professors felt that publications should never be required.

The most frequently cited suggestion for improvement of the scholarly activity of SCDE professors was to provide more released time for such activity. Other suggestions included the need for better research problem selection on the part of the professor, provision of more adequate support assistance, imposition of more rigorous expectations accompanied by tangible rewards, and use of a more appropriate definition of research as it applies to education.

## Professional and University Service

Thirty-five percent of the SCDE professors felt more valued than other professors for their professional and university service; only 5 percent of the non-SCDE professors agreed with this assessment. Fourteen percent of the SCDE professors felt their services less valued than that of other professors in their institution, while only 6 percent of the non-SCDE professors agreed with that assessment.

### Status of Education Professors

Nineteen percent of the SCDE professors felt that the status of the SCDE professor is higher than several years ago. Only 3 percent of the non-SCDE professors agreed with them. Forty-one percent of all of the professors agreed that the current status of the SCDE professors is lower than it was a few years ago. Almost twice as many private college SCDE professors perceived the SCDE professor's status as higher today than did public college professors. Fifty percent of all SCDE professor administrators, compared to 31 percent of the SCDE professor teachers, saw the status of the SCDE professoriate as lower than in past years.

### Job Satisfaction

Sixty-two percent of all professors found greatest job satisfaction in teaching and working with learners. Twenty-six percent of the SCDE professors and 32 percent of the non-SCDE professors found the opportunity to make a contribution and to be influential especially satisfying. Nine percent of all the professors found their greatest satisfaction in writing or research. The greatest work-related frustration cited by SCDE professors included apathy, excessive loads, external interference with the education unit, lack of resources, inability to influence, and organizational dysfunctions. Other frustrations among non-SCDE professors were related to administrative trivia and paperwork, too little money, lack of capable students, collegial infighting, and lack of an understanding administration.

## DISCUSSION

SCDE professors do not choose professorial careers because of a desire to do research. Engaging in research activities is something that many education professors must discipline themselves to do. Research is not viewed as an activity that most aspire to or do with relative ease. Research and writing do not appear to be primary sources of job satisfaction for education professors; teaching and working with learners provide the most satisfaction. Most education professors believe they need more time for research even though they feel they already have considerable control over their time. This suggests that accomplishing more research may be less a matter of available time than it is of setting priorities and electing how to use that time.

SCDE professors agree that writing and research are the most commonly accepted indicators of scholarly activity. However, both SCDE and non-SCDE professors endorse other indicators which are largely process and participatory in nature and which may be categorized as professional service or teaching related. There appears to be a fairly widespread belief among SCDE professors that their scholarly activity should be defined differently than that of other professors and some professional service activities should be included within that definition. The problem may well lie in the failure of the SCDE professor to recognize the scholarly nature of such activities by translating them into a mode that permits them to be analyzed and reported in a scholarly manner.

The majority of education professors report that they are engaged in research and believe that research involvement has a positive effect on teaching quality. From all indications, the frequency of research and writing activity of education professors compares favorably with that of noneducation professors. The majority of SCDE professors have published within the past five years. Virtually all SCDE professors are active in making major presentations and providing professional service. It would appear that the frequency of activity in these two areas is far greater for SCDE professors than for non-SCDE professors. This finding supports the discussion of this matter by Ducharme and Agne (1982).

SCDE professors believe that their work loads are heavier and that more is generally expected of them than of their non-SCDE colleagues. SCDE professors believe they are better teachers than other professors, but do not believe their teaching quality is sufficiently valued by their institutions. Most education professors also see their own teaching ability as better than that of other professors in their field.

Education professors do not view the scholarly activity of their SCDE colleagues as particularly impressive, although they view their own activity as greater than that of others in their field. Most SCDE professors give higher value to the quality of scholarly activity among the colleagues in their own institutions than they acknowledge for SCDE professors as a group. A large portion of SCDE professors view scholarly productivity of education professors as inferior in quality to that of non-SCDE professors. If the scholarly productivity reported by the SCDE professors is accurate, then it would appear that SCDE professors are themselves responsible for promoting a negative image of education professors as scholarly producers.

Many education professors believe the role expectation for them is different from that of other noneducation professors and that it should be different. Most of this belief may stem from the feelings of SCDE professors that their contributions to the institution outside of research and writing are not highly valued, and their research and writing are not as highly valued as that of non-SCDE colleagues. A large portion of both SCDE and non-SCDE believe that the status of SCDE professors is lower today than it was a few years ago. This suggests that there may be a need for the education professor to make a concerted effort to better inform professorial colleagues about the nature of his/her scholarly work.

## CONCLUSION

While the perceptions reported here are based on limited, self-reported information, they are obviously real to the respondents who participated in the study. It appears clear that SCDE professors should examine their individual behaviors and attitudes to determine if they reflect the commitment to scholarship fundamental to professing. Efforts to enhance scholarship and research do not mean that one can afford to be less concerned with teaching competence or professional service responsibilities. On the contrary, scholarship and research can have a positive effect on both teaching and service.

It is also apparent that expectations for SCDE professors are diverse and many. It is critical that professors find ways of responding to these expectations while engaging in scholarly activity at a level commensurate with university expectations. Elevation of the profession of teaching is related to many factors, one of which has to do with the status of schools of education within the higher education community. SCDE professors must be the epitome of excellence in teaching. In addition, SCDE professors must be valued providers of professional service to practitioners if professional schools are to retain their role in teacher preparation. The education professor must value and take pride in the interrelationship between scholarship, teaching, and professional service, and recognize that these activities nurture one another and should not be separated. As Schwebel and others have pointed out, universities no longer permit education professors to concentrate their efforts only on teaching or professional service. More important, research and scholarship are essential for the intellectual vitality of the education professoriate and of schools of education.

Scholarly activity is vital not only because it is highly valued with the university community. If education professors are to contribute to the improvement of teaching and learning and positively influence schooling practices, they must lead the way in educational research. They must be respected scholars, with scholarship defined as including all forms of creative and intellectual productivity. As Wisniewski argues in a later chapter, schools, colleges, and departments of education have the potential for being among the most innovative and intellectually exciting units on any campus. This is possible only if education professors strive toward this ideal and seek to attain the status of respected scholar.

Finally, this study, however tentative, suggests that the difference between SCDE and non-SCDE professors is a matter of degree. Some SCDE professors are meeting the diverse challenge of their calling; others are only partially doing so. The perceptions reported here suggest a reluctance by some SCDE professors to wholeheartedly embrace the scholarly role. Nonetheless, increased scholarly activity is attainable by SCDE professors; it is a legitimate expectation.

## REFERENCES

Bok,D. (1986). *Higher Learning*. Cambridge, Mass: Harvard University Press.

Ducharme, E. R. (1985). Establishing the place of teacher education in the university. *Journal of Teacher Education, 36* (4), 8–11.

_____ & Agne, R. (1982). The education professoriate: A research-based perspective. *Journal of Teacher Education, 33* (6), 30–36.

Lanier, J. (1984). The preservice teacher education improvement project: A critical review. *Journal of Teacher Education, 35* (4), 24–28.

Schwebel, M. (1982). Research productivity of education faculty: A comparative study. *Educational Studies, 13,* 224–39.

*Yearbook of Higher Education.* (1982–83) 14th Ed. Chicago: Marquis Professional Publications.

# 7

# A Plight of Teacher Educators: Clinical Mentalities in a Scientific Culture

JAMES RATHS
LILIAN KATZ
AMY MCANINCH

## INTRODUCTION

Snow (1959) describes the cleavage between the two cultures of science and the humanities within the university community. Actually, university communities are far more diverse in their orientations. Many more than two cultures coexist in every university setting. University faculty primarily engaged in training functions, including teacher educators (see Authors' Notes, 1), have come to know and appreciate two particular cultures endemic to the university community and profoundly influential in their lives (Judge, 1982; Kimble,

1984; Sergiovanni, 1985). One of these cultures is associated with the world of the researcher, the scientist, who seeks to understand and generate new knowledge. The second has to do with the arena of the practitioner, the trainer, the developer, who applies knowledge to complex and demanding individual cases and in turn trains others to do the same.

This essay focuses on the impacts of the clash between these two cultures on the lives of teacher educators, recognizing that many others within the university community are affected by it. Subcultures coexist in many locations within the university. As Dearden (1983) reminds us,

> . . . the relation between theory and practice causes puzzlement across a very wide field. How is economics related to running a business, jurisprudence to being a lawyer, theology to faith, ethics to conduct, logic to reasoning, or for that matter, sociology to being a police inspector? (p. 5)

These two coexisting worlds are quite disparate. Schwab (1978), in inquiring into these distinctions but with different rubrics, asserts:

> The radical difference of the practical from the theoretic mode is visible in the fact that it differs from the theoretic not in one aspect but in many: It differs from the theoretic in method. Its problems originate from a different source. Its subject matter is of a distinctly different character. Its outcome is of a different kind (p. 288).

The cultures have different folkways, embrace different values, address different challenges, and require different mentalities on the part of their actors. Both realms are critical to the functioning of the university as a locus of efforts to carry out research, service, and teaching, but their mutual commitment to the ends advanced by the university does not diminish the tensions that exist between members of the two groups.

Freidson (1972) documents the existence of this particular cultural division of the university community in his study of the sociology of the medical profession. He suggests that medical practitioners have a different orientation to their work than medical researchers. In fact, he asserts that this disparity in mindset extends well beyond the world of work and is manifested in contrasting views of the world. In sum, persons devoted to service and to practice think differently about problems, have different norms, use different problem solving patterns than do those who are committed primarily to research.

*Clinical mentality* and *scientific mentality* are not normative terms (see Authors' Notes, 2). In our culture, the values ascribed to almost anything labeled *Scientific* suggest that the *clinical* label may have derogatory connotations. That is not the thrust of Freidson's work nor of this essay. The terms are meant to be descriptive and neutral.

Our descriptions of the major attributes of the clinical and scientific mentalities are based on extrapolations from Freidson's work. We close with some implications our analysis holds for the organization and administration of teacher education.

According to Freidson, at least five attributes differentiate clinical and scientific mentalities: readiness to act; confidence; source of justifications; search for knowledge; and uses of knowledge. Each of these attributes, summarized in Table I, is discussed below.

**Table 1**
Distinctions between Scientists and Practitioners in
Orientations to Knowledge, Research, and Practice
Clinical Mentalities

| *Scientific Orientation* | *Clinical Orientation* |
| --- | --- |
| Reflective: Inclined to seek further information. | Active: Is wont to act |
| Skeptical: Concerned with adequacy of methods and robustness of data. | Confident: Believes in efficacy of the available procedures. |
| Theoretical: Wants to build system of concepts and explanations that make sense. | Pragmatic: Concerned primarily with whether something will "work". |
| Scholarly: Reads research of others. | Empirical: Relies on personal experiences. |
| Uniformity of Nature: Strives to uncover laws that account for phenomena. | Uniqueness of Nature: Believes phenomena in real world too complex to be lawful. |

Concepts here based on Freidson's (1972) work.

## READINESS TO ACT

Individuals with clinical mentalities feel compelled to act when faced with a problem or a demanding client. They are unlikely to study the problem further, to collect more data, to read up on the peculiarities of a particular case. Individuals with scientific mentalities, in contrast, almost always resist rushing into action, holding that reflective and deliberate thought is the proper response before acting in a problematic situation. Thus, researchers tend to review the alternatives for action, explore each option's indicators and counterindicators, and consult with others before acting. The penchant to act versus the wont to deliberate differentiates the clinical mentality from the scientific.

## CONFIDENCE

Practitioners tend to have confidence in the efficacy of their interventions. They are ready to persuade on-lookers of the rightness of their practices even in the absence of robust evidence and, in fact, feel insulted when others dare to challenge the claims made for what has been done in practice. Scientists, on the other hand, are inclined to doubt any claims and call for data whenever conclusions seem too optimistic and sanguine. Scientists are disposed to ask "How do you know?" Doubt characterizes the mood of scientists in the face of a practical problem.

## SOURCE OF JUSTIFICATION

Clinicians often claim that the efficacy of an intervention or a technique is justified because "it works" (Denemark & Nutter, 1984, p. 206). Scientists are generally suspicious of such a crude form of pragmatism. They are more interested in "how" the intervention worked, with the credibility of the claim that an intervention "ought" to work based on a particular model or paradigm that accounts for changes in the variables included within its scope. While practitioners justify a proposed intervention on empirical grounds, scientists want to have a theoretical explanation of the empirical data to vouch for its legitimacy as a professional practice.

## SEARCH FOR KNOWLEDGE

Clinicians are not wont to turn to scientific literature to acquire professional knowledge. Instead, much of their knowledge comes from personal, firsthand experiences. As Freidson (1972) says,

> Indeed, the consulting professions in general and medicine in particular encourage the limitation of perspective by its members through ideological emphasis on the importance of first hand, individual experience and on individual freedom to make choices and to act on the basis of such experiences. Such emphasis is directly contrary to the emphasis of science on shared knowledge, collected and tested on the basis of methods meant to overcome the deficiencies of individual experience (p. 347).

Scientists place more confidence in the professional literature, in the findings of research and the scholarly analyses of colleagues in the field.

## USES OF KNOWLEDGE

While scientists seek to discover laws or principles with broad applicability to practice, clinicians are convinced that it is a fruitless search. They often view each case in practice as unique. Therefore, general rules or principles will not be of help to the practitioner. While scientists generate production functions or describe treatment effects by charting differences between sample means, clinicians act on the belief that an intervention works with differential effects. They are less interested in the overall, mean effect than in the way a particular individual responds to it.

Freidson claims these aspects of mentality are mutually dependent and related. For example, the suspicion of law-like principles discourages clinicians from relying on published research, and instead encourages them to place confidence in personal experiences. Similarly, the mutually reinforcing aspects of seeing something work weakens the disposition to inquire into the theoretical aspects of the intervention.

## FUNCTIONALITY OF THE CLINICAL MENTALITY

Is it "poor practice" not to adopt a scientific rationality when practicing a profession, whether it be business, medicine, or teaching? Freidson (1972) answers this question in the negative by arguing that:

> The [clinical] rationality is particularized and technical; it is a method of sorting the enormous mass of concrete detail confronting [the professional] in his individual cases. The difference between clinical rationality and scientific rationality is that

clinical rationality is not a tool for the exploration or discovery of general principles, as is the scientific method, but only a tool for sorting the interconnections of perceived and hypothesized facts (p. 171).

In short, being clinical is far from acting unprofessionally; quite the contrary, the dispositions which constitute this mentality are professionally highly valuable to individuals working in clinical settings.

At this point, our argument takes two turns from Freidson's work. First, we will spend the rest of this chapter discussing teaching and not medicine. Clearly, the professions of medicine and education are quite different; however, we think the two professions are similar in significant ways. Both deal with individuals in complex settings that press for action. Some evidence suggests that teachers adopt a mentality very similar to that attributed to the clinicians in Freidson's study (Doyle & Ponder, 1977–78, pp. 6ff).

The second turn is from teaching to teacher education. Eventually, we want to discuss the mentalities of teacher educators. We are convinced that mentalities are determined in large measure by the press of contexts in the world of work. The demands of teaching shape professor's mentalities and thus affect their preparation of teachers. If our argument is convincing, then our claim that teacher educators are more likely to possess clinical outlooks than their colleagues in the foundations of education, where classroom experience is less likely a criterion of employment, will also be compelling.

If teacher educators are more "clinical" in their outlooks than their colleagues in the education professoriate, how did they get that way? The task of teaching school, generally a prerequisite for becoming a teacher educator, shapes the thinking habits of those engaged in the practice of public school teaching. In the following section we describe characteristics of the contexts in which teachers, some of whom are to become teacher educators, practice their profession. These qualities, including complexity of the the task, the isolation of the classroom, and the state of the available research relevant to coping with the enduring problems of teaching make clinical mentalities functional in the school setting.

## COMPLEXITY OF THE CLASSROOM

Only recently have researchers begun to understand the complexity of the teacher's life in the classroom. The emergent literature on the sociology of classrooms provides an explanation for the functionality of the "clinical mentality" for teachers working under constraining organizational conditions and meeting the pressing tasks of instruction and classroom management.

Far from the simple places classrooms were assumed to be until about twenty-five years ago, classrooms are now characterized as busy, crowded, and constraining. As Dreeben (1973) points out:

> Classrooms, where conscripted children are gathered in confined spaces over long spans of time, engender problems of compliance and order for teachers. From the teacher's perspective, the central issue is engaging pupils in the instructional proceedings—keeping them interested, at work and actively involved. The means for doing so, however, are not well understood so that one often finds teachers attempting to keep up with and control the rapid flow of events; in part the director of these events, in part the prisoner, but in any case deeply engrossed by them. . . . With the endemic uncertainty and unpredictability of classroom life, the teacher, in attempting to instruct and maintain order, becomes more the reactor to than the designer of classroom activities (pp. 450ff).

Many writers have discussed the isolation of the classroom teacher. One implication of the isolation is that the success or failure experienced by a teacher is often taken as a measure of that particular teacher's effort. That is, there is no one with whom to share responsibility when something fails. Any failures are not the school's failure or the district's failure but the teacher's failure. In this setting, is there any wonder why teachers exhibit a disdain for being second guessed, and why they cannot and do not entertain doubt about the efficacy of their interventions and methods? Expressions of doubt suggest they do not know what they are doing. And the persons who can least entertain doubt are those for whom uncertainty is most painful. How could teachers, thrust into situations such as this, not help but see the world in clinical terms as described by Freidson?

Regardless of the way particular teachers balance all the imperatives of the job, the main point is that they must act. The job demands immediate actions and reactions, frequently in the face of uncertainty and unpredictability. Thus, the acid test of any action, under these pressing conditions is, "Does it work in this case?" The fact that teachers often have to make decisions quickly in a complex environment suggests that intuition, "acting on one's instincts," developing the ability to act on a gut level, becomes highly functional. There is little time to pause, to reflect, to ponder, to be, in effect, scientific.

## LACK OF RELIABLE AND USABLE RESEARCH

There is no "How To Do It" manual for teachers that is the equivalent of the physicians's *Merck Manual*. Standard procedures for coping with the enduring problems of teaching are notably absent. With no firm guidelines based in research or science to guide them, teachers find reflection, the consideration of alternatives, the search through books and research literature, or the consultation with "experts" to be time-consuming and nonproductive. For example, how can teachers apply the research supported causal generalization of the form, "Treatment X causes an increase in arithmetic achievement," when the data surely show that in the experiment that spawned the generalization, not all children gained; some actually lost proficiency when, disregarding means, the patterns of individual student gains and losses are taken into account. To tell teachers to rely on mean scores is to disregard their outlook about the teaching task, in short, their mentality.

Without reliable evidence and under the compelling need to act, teachers must have the courage to try something out to "see if it works." Freidson termed this approach *crude pragmatism*. And because few guides, few generalizations, few principles of scientific merit are available to them, teachers create personal principles. As Freidson (1972) recounts:

> 'Principles' are generated in the course of clinical practice, but they are the generalizations from clinical experience, which is to say, generalization from personal and systematically biased experience. As Oken (1961) has stated, 'clinical experience' is frequently personal mythology based upon one or two incidents or on stories by colleagues' (pp. 171–72).

Tversky and Kahneman (1974) demonstrate the way individuals, and presumably professionals, when compelled to make judgments under certain conditions, rarely find analysis a functional approach. Instead, they work to simplify complex tasks by relying on a number of heuristic principles that are found to be useful.

## CONSEQUENCES ACCRUING TO THOSE WITH
## CLINICAL MENTALITIES IN A UNIVERSITY SETTING

In the previous section, we suggested that clinical mentality is linked to the conditions under which teachers work. Turning now to higher education, we believe that university personnel, such as teacher educators who prepare others for clinical roles, are more likely to possess clinical mentalities than their colleagues who are less engaged in training functions.

Our assertion is based on several considerations. First, teacher educators are far more likely to have been recruited from the ranks of classroom teachers than are those who are engaged in research. The findings of Carter (1984) and Ducharme and Agne (1982) support the generalization that most teacher educators were, at one time, teachers in the schools. While it is the case that some may have left the school because, in part, they resisted adopting a clinical mentality and thus found teaching to be unmanageable or dissatisfying, those who came into clinical positions on a teacher education faculty may be likely to have clinical mentalities.

Second, while surely all professors are, as teachers, thrust regularly into a clinical role, for the researcher, teaching does not represent a heavy emotional investment. Researchers are not often affected professionally by the quality of their classroom teaching. They are generally rewarded predominately for journal articles published or funds generated through proposal writing. Because the emotional commitment to teaching is comparatively weak, the press to become clinical when pondering the teaching act is less acute. Professors in these straits can distance themselves from the enduring problems of teaching. To a large degree, they can avoid issues of assessment, of being prepared, of being relevant. There is little call to take on clinical attitudes. On the contrary, to be successful in the scientific world of research, the attitudes and mentalities of the scientist are required.

Third, teacher educators are often primarily responsible for instruction in methods courses and supervision of field internships. In teaching methods courses, teacher educators focus more heavily on "how-to" aspects of various techniques than their theoretical bases. Because practice is the primary concern of methods courses, teacher educators focus on such clinical issues as taking action and "what works," thereby adopting the clinical point of view. Furthermore, because teacher educators frequently are responsible for supervision of field experience, they are in closer contact with the public schools and with teachers than their colleagues and must prepare candidates to function in public schools. The task then reinforces the mentality teacher educators are likely to have brought from their previous public school roles.

Consequently, teacher educators are more likely to be clinically oriented for many of the reasons associated with their previous work roles as classroom teachers. The question is then, what happens to persons who manifest clinical mentalities in the university setting?

## ATTITUDES TOWARD RESEARCH

One attribute of the clinical mentality is an impatience with research reports and research findings, especially those of a statistical nature. Individuals who work day in and day out with a variety of persons may not be interested in reports of central tendency or estimates of variance explained. They need to know what to do with the individuals in front of them. There is a little research that can tell them what to do. From this perspective, teacher educators often show their disdain for research and for the research process. They generally do not engage in research; they find it uninformative. Furthermore, they share negative views about research with their colleagues. Some mimic the ten minute rituals at the AERA meetings and laugh at the sophistication they consider "pseudo" found in the research reports published in the *American Educational Research Journal*. Their generalized lack of respect for research and their abstention from research redounds against them. Prizing research is a "norm" of the academy, and being derisive of such a norm engenders serious sanctions, both informal and formal.

## CLAIMS OF EFFICACY

One element of the clinical mentality is a powerful confidence in the efficacy of the interventions and other actions in which one is engaged. Because few standards of conduct are found and great difficulty exists in defending many of the decisions instructors make, those with clinical mentalities make assessments of their own effectiveness based on what they see and the way things work out. Most of them are positive. Researchers defend the quality of their work by counting the number of journal articles published or the number of dollars brought to the college or university through grant-writing efforts. When teacher educators present data on their efficacy, they ask that their teaching be recognized as high quality, and often are distraught when the act of teaching is seen as having little value unless its quality can be demonstrated. Of course, the quality is demonstrated to the instructors themselves by what they see day in and day out. But there is some difficulty in communicating this quality to faculty committees allocating merit salary increases, hence the teacher educator is often very low on the merit list. The evidence that seems relevant in making salary merit decisions to those with clinical mentalities is rejected by those who think "scientifically."

## DIFFICULTY IN EXCHANGING VIEWS

We have characterized the distinctions between these two mentalities as cultural ones. Nowhere is that analogy more apt than in efforts for members of these two "sects" to communicate with one another. It is similar to persons from different cultures trying to share their views. Each fails to speak the language of the other, and, instead of responding to apparent dissonance with wonderment or with additional effort to listen more carefully or speak with greater precision, the participants tend to become angry and disrespectful.

In sum, the clinical mentality faculty are seen as "norm breakers." They place little value on research, they do not engage in research, they do not apply research. As is the case in any organization, those who break the norms, or are perceived as norm breakers, are sanctioned.

## IMPLICATIONS

We have painted a grim picture. The tensions between these particular orientations surely affect teacher educators' feelings of satisfaction with their work, their sense of efficacy, and their reputations. And as Kimble (1984) remarked, the prospects for achieving harmony are not bright (p. 833). At least three implications must be considered if our descriptions are at all accurate.

First, teacher educators must become bicultural. They will need to communicate in the cultures of both mentalities, respecting the norms and customs of both. Katz et al. (1982) carried out a study of the reputations of teacher educators and found that, by and large, the professors of a large midwestern university saw teacher educators as being overly interested in the nitty-gritty of schools, too involved in practical matters to inquire into school problems with rigor. On the other hand, practicing teachers saw teacher educators as being involved in model building, theory testing and writing research grants. While both sets of reputations were different, both were perjorative. There is a need on the part of teacher educators to switch the reputations this study suggested were held of them. They must be seen as researchers and scholars by university faculty, and as practitioners by the teachers in the community.

At present, some exceptional teacher educators "pass" in both cultures. It would be desirable to do case studies, to find out how some individuals succeed in both places, while at the same time studying those who excel in only one of the arenas. A series of such studies would be instructive.

Second, the effectiveness of teacher educators is hindered by the divisiveness and stress they experience on university campuses due in part to cultural conflict. Clearly, one alternative is to assign teacher education functions to a special purpose institution removed from university settings. In such contexts, perhaps teacher educators would be better able to carry out their roles as trainers of teachers. In short, this recommendation is a call for a return to the normal school. Normal schools enjoyed a clear mission, and the resources assigned to teacher education were utilized on its behalf. Now, teacher education does not receive its share of the university budget, and the more glamorous research efforts are the ones that receive high priority, not perhaps on graduation day when the parents of undergraduates are in the audience, but on the occasion when the budgets are framed and pay raises are determined (Peseau & Orr, 1980). Perhaps separation is an option that needs further study, especially given the analysis presented in this chapter.

A third, more modest, implication should be considered. If it is impractical for historical and practical reasons to reopen normal schools, perhaps teacher educators and teacher education programs should be isolated at the university, with their own school and their own budgets. Functioning like law schools or medical schools, schools of teacher education could stop fencing with senate committees or with the politics of academic affairs found within the college structure. This suggestion does not assume that law or medical schools are not engaged in campus politics. They do not, however, have to negotiate as fervently to change curricula or to reward professors who make significant contributions in arenas not recognized by a vice-chancellor for academic affairs. Organized under administrators sympathetic to the education of professions, colleges and schools of teacher education would be in a better position to chart their destinies without worrying about the annual sanctions delivered to them by those colleagues who are disdainful of training as a function and who prize only the production of scholarly work.

## REFERENCES

Carter, H. (1984). Teachers of teachers. In L. G. Katz & J. D. Raths (Eds.) *Advances in teacher education*, Vol. 1. Norwood, N.J.: Ablex Publishing Corp.

Dearden, R. F. (1983). *Theory and practice in education*. London: Routledge & Kegan.

Denemark, G. W., & Nutter, N. (1984). The case for extended programs of initial teacher preparation. In L. G. Katz & J. D. Raths, (Eds.), *Advances in teacher education*, Vol. 1 (pp. 203–46). Norwood, N.J.: Ablex Publishing Corp.

Dreeben, R. (1973). The school as workplace. In R. M. W. Travers (Ed.), *Second handbook of research on teaching* (pp. 450–73). Chicago: Rand McNally

Doyle, W., & Ponder, G. A. (1977–78). The practicality ethic in teacher decision making. *Interchange, 8* (3), 1–12.

Ducharme, E. R., & Agne, R. M. (1982). Education professoriate: A research-based perspective. *Journal of Teacher Education, 33* (6), 30–36.

Freidson, E. (1972). *Profession of medicine*. New York: Dodd, Mead and Company.

Judge, H. (1982). *American graduate schools of education*. New York: The Ford Foundation.

Katz, L. G., Raths, J. D., Irving, J., Kurachi, A., Mohanty, C., & Soni, M. (1982, March). *Reputations of teacher educators among members of their role set*. Paper presented at the annual meeting of the American Educational Research Association, New York City.

Kimble, G. A. (1984). Psychology's two cultures. *American Psychologist, 39* (8), 833–839.

Oken, D. (1961). What to tell cancer patients: A study of medical attitudes. *Journal of the American Medical Association, 175,* 1120–28.

Peseau, B. A., & Orr, P. G. (1980). The outrageous underfunding of teacher education. *Phi Delta Kappan, 62* (2), 100–02.

Schwab, J. J. (1978). The practical: A language for curriculum. In I. Westbury & N. J. Wilkof (Eds.), *Science, curriculum and liberal education: Selected essays,* (pp. 287–321). Chicago: University of Chicago Press.

Sergiovanni, T. J. (1985). Landscapes, mindscapes, and reflective practice in supervision. *Journal of Curriculum and Supervision, 1,* 5–17.

Snow, C. P. (1959). *The two cultures and the scientific revolution.* London: Cambridge University Press.

Tversky, A., & Kahneman, D. (1974). Judgment under uncertainty: Heuristics and biases. *Science, 185* (Sept.), 1124–31.

*AUTHORS' NOTES*

1. While the contributors to this volume discuss professors of education in a generic sense, we have analyzed a particular subset, *viz,* the teacher educators. This qualification or delimitation is significant for anyone seeking to integrate the observations and suggestions found in this chapter with those advanced in the other chapters.

2. Several critics of earlier drafts of this paper have called us to task for using the term *mentality* to describe teacher educators' orientation to their work. A number of our colleagues felt it had a pejorative connotation, as though mentalities were normally thought to be negative, or that having a mentality in and of itself suggests that the teacher educator in question is somehow less of a person, is an individual out of control, or in the throes of some sort of spell. As we have made plain, our essay is based firmly on the work of E. Freidson (1972), and it seems important for us to use his term to properly acknowledge his contribution to our thinking. Of course, Professor Freidson bears no responsibility for the interpretations we have made of his writing.

# 8

# The Uses of Time:
## Evocations of an Ethos

### HENDRIK D. GIDEONSE

Many issues and topics are addressed in this book, all of which seek to probe and describe the ethos of schools of education. What is the fundamental character of such schools? What is the milieu in which professors work and from which they receive explicit and implicit signals regarding their behaviors, productivity, worth, and stature? However difficult the task of finding answers to such questions, one point is clear: whatever is done by professors takes time. Examining the way a professor spends time is one approach to evoking the ethos of a college. Of particular interest is the way time usage reveals the extent to which scholarship is important in that ethos.

Certification and accreditation standards, for example, emphasize the instructional demands of training efforts. The heavy emphasis on classroom instruction and the lack of resources for clinical programs are often blamed for the lessened attention to inquiry that characterizes schools and colleges of education (Tucker, 1981). Other factors have been suggested. Severe critics posit the low intellectual capacity of the education professoriate to carry out such work. Some teacher educators cite the heavy time demands of field-based instructional programs. Others might suggest a preference for working with people directly rather than on analytic tasks associated with research.

No one really knows the reasons for the lower emphasis on inquiry and scholarship, in part because no one has studied the education professoriate in a way to be able to make grounded statements. This pilot study began out of simple curiosity about how much time education faculty devote to scholarship and other activities. What might the allocation of time to professorial tasks reveal about the ethos of schools of education; what might be revealed about the way faculty define their roles and responsibilities?

This chapter offers no conclusions about the professoriate. The data presented should not be extrapolated to any specific campus or to the education professoriate as a whole. Hopefully, the discussion will stimulate other questions about what professors do and perhaps ought to do in each reader's setting. It is offered solely as a stimulus to thought about the professoriate.

## METHODOLOGY

During 1984 and 1985, faculty from three teacher education institutions were invited to participate in a pilot study of the way faculty allocate their time. The institutions are described below. Faculty who participated were all volunteers. They kept logs of their activities. Each participant was assured of confidentiality in the reporting of results.

Twenty-seven faculty completed logs: ten on one campus, twelve on the second, and five on the third. Each participant was given a notebook small enough to fit in a purse or shirt pocket. Participants were asked to keep track of their time for one seven-day week. They were asked to account for their time each day from waking in the morning to turning in at night. Personal time was to be recorded with the simple designation *Personal*. All professional time was to be recorded by briefly identifying specific activities. Every time participants changed their activity, they were asked to record the new activity and the time of the shift. Thus, the respective time allocations to each could be calculated.

The logs were transcribed into a common format; the amount of time allocated to each activity was calculated. Based on two readings of the logs, a fourteen-category schema for the activities was developed. On a third analysis of the transcribed materials, each block of activity was coded within the schema. While the "n" is too small to support statistical analysis, the findings are intriguing.

## DATA CATEGORIES

The fourteen identified categories of faculty activity are somewhat arbitrary. A category had to be found for every professional activity reported. For example, a journal entry *Attended class* was judged, in part because of other clues internal to the log, to mean *Taught class*. There could be fewer or more categories, as will quickly be apparent. The categories embraced the following activities:

1. *Preparation for class* including setting up equipment, reading, preparing handouts, reviewing notes, and similar activities. Also coded here were any entries referencing general professional reading, professional development, or post-doctoral study.
2. *Scheduled class instruction.*
3. *Evaluation of student performance* (with the exception of number 4 below).
4. *Doctoral instruction,* anything having to do with the non-scheduled class dimensions of doctoral study, such as committee responsibilities, conferences, defenses, dissertation reviews.
5. *Supervision of practica,* such as student teaching, internships.
6. *Travel* associated with supervision of practica or class instruction off-campus.
7. *Research and scholarship.*
8. *Governance* including service on college and university committees and senates.
9. *Public service* associated with professional associations.
10. *Public service* associated with schools.
11. *Other public services,* such as community agencies, governmental bodies.
12. *Student advising* (with the exception of doctoral advising assigned to number 4 above).
13. *Administrative duties,* a catch-all, including miscellaneous phone calls, answering mail, admitting students, computing advanced standings, program meetings, program planning, personnel matters, program evaluation.
14. *Ceremonial responsibilities,* including receptions, commencement-related activities, celebrations of doctoral defenses, retirement parties.

Each faculty log was coded to retain identification with each of the three campuses. Analysis of the logs revealed great diversity in the allocation of faculty time to a variety of activities. Tabulations were made to determine the number of minutes spent on each activity over the seven-day period. A percentage was calculated based on the total time devoted to professional activities each week by each respondent. Table I displays the variations in time allocated across the twenty-seven faculty to each type of activity.

In Table II, the fourteen categories are aggregated into five composite categories: instruction, scholarship, advising, service, and administration/governance. In each category, respondents are rank ordered according to the total number of minutes reported for each activity. The average number of hours of the activity is further summarized into low, middle, and high categories.

Table III compares the average percentages of time to the five major categories by respondents at each of the campuses. Other tables were developed in the course of the analysis, but the three tables reproduced here are sufficient to summarize the primary findings of this exploratory study.

## ANALYSIS

Chief among the observations is the high degree of commitment shown by these faculty to their responsibilities. The average professional work week exceeds fifty-seven hours. Individual faculty manifest dramatically different patterns of time allocation. Some of the difference is a function of role. At least one of the faculty members was a department head while other faculty members held program coordination responsibilities.

The major portion of the variation seems to be a function of personal and professional style. Apart from meeting classes and keeping scheduled office hours, faculty have some latitude in allocating their work effort. The wide variation in time expended on instruction is only partially accounted for by variations in the number of classes each is assigned to teach. For all twenty-seven faculty, the average instructional load was 6.5 class/credit hours; 7.85 hours for the high seven; 7.4 hours for the middle seven; and 4.9 hours for the low seven. Far greater differences exist between the average clock hours invested in preparation for instruction and the actual teaching: 39.4 for the high seven, 19.6 for the middle seven, and 8.6 for the low seven. This wide variation cannot be accounted for by the differences in scheduled class teaching assignments.

**Table I**
Ranges and Average Expenditures of
Faculty Time in Hours by Category

| | Individual Faculty Ranged from | | The AVERAGE Expended by |
| | a LOW of | to a HIGH of | All Faculty Was |
|---|---|---|---|
| *Teaching* | | | |
| Class preparation | 0.5 | 21.80 | 6.2 |
| Scheduled teaching | 0.0 | 15.30 | 6.8 |
| Evaluation of | 0.0 | | |
| student performance | 0.0 | 24.80 | 5.6 |
| Doctoral teaching | 0.0 | 16.30 | 2.8[1] |
| Practicum supervision | 0.0 | 12.80 | 1.5 |
| Travel to practica | 0.0 | 6.50 | 1.5 |
| *Scholarly Activity* | 0.0 | 35.50 | 9.0 |
| *Governance* | 0.0 | 5.50 | 1.5 |
| *Service* | | | |
| Professional associations | 0.0 | 2.50 | 0.3 |
| Schools | 0.0 | 7.30 | 1.2 |
| Other agencies | 0.0 | 9.70 | 1.9 |
| Advising | 0.0 | 10.77 | 4.8 |
| Administrative Duties | 0.4 | 35.20 | 12.3 |
| Ceremonial Functions | 0.0 | 11.50 | 2.0 |
| *Overall* | | | |
| All faculty | 42.1 | 88.30 | 57.2[2] |
| Seven faculty with lowest total hours | 42.1 | 48.20 | 45.3 |
| Mid seven faculty | 50.00 | 58.5 | 55.8 |
| Seven faculty with highest total hours | 63.9 | 88.30 | 72.5 |

[1]Average based on twenty-two cases because one campus did not offer doctoral level work.
[2]Total of individual categories .2 higher due to rounding.

The analytic device (Table II) of dividing the twenty-seven into three subgroups corresponding to the low, middle, and high seven of the total distribution yields additional information about the diversity and range of time allocations. In each of the five types of activity (instruction, scholarship, advising, service, and administration/ governance) the differences in time allocated by faculty in each sub- group are not merely a matter of a few percentage points. The high and middle group allocations of time to each activity are substantially higher than for the low groups. The most dramatic differences appear in the area of scholarship. But the differences for preparation/ instruction, given the far smaller variance in assigned teaching loads, are equally startling.

Table III suggests the diversity that may exist in the missions of the three colleges. The following characterizations may be helpful in reviewing the data reported.

## Table II
### Rank Orderings of Faculty by Hour Allocations to Functional Categories

| | Instruction[1] | | (Class Hours) (f) | Scholarship[2] | | | Advising[3] | | | Service[4] | | | Admin/Governance[5] | | |
|---|---|---|---|---|---|---|---|---|---|---|---|---|---|---|---|
| | Hours | Rank | | | Hours | Rank | | Hours | Rank | | Hours | Rank | | Hours | Rank |
| A9 | 62.7 | –1 | –9 | B9 | 43.0 | –1 | C5 | 10.7 | –1 | C1 | 9.7 | –1 | B10 | 35.3 | –1 |
| C1 | 46.1 | –2 | –8 | A3 | 37.9 | –2 | A2 | 10.1 | –2 | B9 | 8.5 | –2 | B8 | 31.5 | –2 |
| C4 | 39.9 | –3 | –9 | A4 | 35.5 | –3 | C4 | 9.0 | –3 | A1 | 7.7 | –3 | B11 | 28.3 | –3 |
| B11 | 35.2 | –4 | –5 | A8 | 20.2 | –4 | A5 | 8.8 | –4 | C2 | 7.3 | –4 | A5 | 23.5 | –4 |
| A10 | 31.2 | –5 | –11 | A10 | 19.9 | –5 | C2 | 6.7 | –5 | A6 | 7.3 | –4 | B12 | 21.9 | –5 |
| B5 | 30.3 | –6 | –7 | B2 | 18.3 | –6 | B1 | 6.5 | –6 | B4 | 7.3 | –4 | B4 | 21.7 | –6 |
| B6 | 30.3 | –6 | –6 | B4 | 17.5 | –7 | B7 | 6.3 | –7 | B2 | 5.5 | –7 | B6 | 20.1 | –7 |
| C3 | 28.4 | –8 | –6 | A5 | 14.8 | –8 | B10 | 5.9 | –8 | B3 | 4.8 | –8 | A1 | 20.1 | –7 |
| B1 | 27.2 | –9 | –3 | A7 | 13.5 | –9 | C3 | 5.5 | –9 | B8 | 4.7 | –9 | A2 | 17.9 | –9 |
| A5 | 26.0 | –10 | –9 | B10 | 10.8 | –10 | B3 | 5.5 | –9 | B11 | 4.6 | –10 | C3 | 17.3 | –10 |
| B3 | 24.9 | –11 | –10 | A2 | 9.0 | –11 | B11 | 5.4 | –11 | C3 | 3.9 | –11 | A7 | 13.4 | –11 |
| A3 | 21.0 | –12 | –8 | C2 | 8.3 | –12 | A9 | 5.3 | –12 | C5 | 3.5 | –12 | B7 | 12.8 | –12 |
| A6 | 20.8 | –13 | –10 | A6 | 8.0 | –13 | B6 | 5.0 | –13 | B12 | 3.3 | –13 | C5 | 11.4 | –13 |
| B7 | 20.3 | –14 | –7 | A9 | 7.3 | –14 | B12 | 4.6 | –14 | A3 | 3.0 | –14 | A8 | 11.1 | –14 |
| B2 | 17.4 | –15 | –6 | B5 | 7.1 | –15 | A1 | 4.6 | –14 | A7 | 2.8 | –15 | A9 | 11.0 | –15 |
| C5 | 16.8 | –16 | –8 | B12 | 7.1 | –15 | A4 | 4.4 | –16 | C4 | 2.3 | –16 | A4 | 11.0 | –15 |
| A2 | 16.1 | –17 | –3 | B7 | 5.5 | –17 | B5 | 4.3 | –17 | B10 | 1.6 | –17 | C2 | 10.3 | –17 |
| C2 | 15.7 | –18 | –8 | C4 | 4.5 | –18 | B8 | 3.9 | –18 | A8 | 1.5 | –18 | A6 | 10.1 | –18 |
| A7 | 15.5 | –19 | –3 | C3 | 4.2 | –19 | B4 | 3.4 | –19 | B5 | 1.3 | –19 | B3 | 9.6 | –19 |
| B8 | 15.0 | –20 | –6 | B11 | 3.3 | –20 | A7 | 2.8 | –20 | A2 | 1.1 | –20 | B2 | 9.0 | –20 |
| B9 | 13.5 | –21 | –7 | B1 | 2.2 | –21 | B9 | 2.5 | –21 | B6 | 0.5 | –21 | C1 | 6.4 | –21 |
| B12 | 10.5 | –22 | –6 | C5 | 1.5 | –22 | A10 | 2.5 | –21 | B7 | 0 | –22 | B1 | 6.0 | –22 |
| A1 | 9.9 | –23 | –6 | A1 | 1.1 | –23 | A6 | 2.1 | –23 | B1 | 0 | –22 | C4 | 2.8 | –23 |
| B4 | 8.7 | –24 | –6 | C1 | 1.0 | –24 | C1 | 1.9 | –24 | A4 | 0 | –22 | A10 | 2.7 | –24 |

| | | | | | | | | | | | | | | | |
|---|---|---|---|---|---|---|---|---|---|---|---|---|---|---|---|
| A4 | 8.4 | -25 | -6 | B3 | 0.8 | -25 | A3 | 1.0 | -25 | A5 | 0 | -22 | B5 | 2.3 | -25 |
| A8 | 8.3 | -26 | -3 | B6 | 0.1 | -26 | A8 | 0.3 | -26 | A9 | 0 | -22 | B9 | 1.0 | -26 |
| B10 | 0.6 | -27 | -0 | B8 | 0.0 | -27 | B2 | 0.0 | -27 | A10 | 0 | -22 | A3 | 1.0 | -26 |

*Average Hours Invested (Assigned Class Hours)*

| | | | | | |
|---|---|---|---|---|---|
| Low Seven | 8.6 (4.9) | 1.0 | 1.5 | .1 | 3.3 |
| Middle Seven | 19.6 (7.4) | 7.5 | 4.8 | 2.9 | 10.1 |
| High Seven | 39.4 (7.9) | 27.5 | 8.3 | 7.6 | 26.0 |
| All 27 | 22.2 (6.5) | 11.2 | 4.8 | 3.4 | 13.7 |

[1]Includes categories #1, 2, 3, 5, and 6.

[2]Includes categories #4 and 7.

[3]Category #12.

[4]Includes categories #9, 10, and 11.

[5]Includes categories #8 and 13.

[6]Assigned class hours were determined by totaling the number of hours spent teaching classes.

[7]Category #12.

**Table III**

Percentage of Faculty Time Allocated to Five Major Activities

|  | Instruction[1] | Scholarship[2] | Advising[3] | Service[4] | Admin./Gov.[5] |
|---|---|---|---|---|---|
| College A | 37.3 | 28.6 | 7.1 | 4.0 | 20.8 |
| College B | 34.7 | 17.3 | 8.0 | 6.2 | 29.8 |
| College C | 51.0 | 6.8 | 11.7 | 9.3 | 16.7 |

[1]Includes categories #1, 2, 3, 5, and 6.
[2]Includes categories #4 and 7.
[3]Category #12.
[4]Includes categories #9, 10, and 11.
[5]Includes categories #8 and 13.

College A is a private institution in the Midwest. It has seventy full-time faculty members in education, serves 1,500 full-time equivalent students at the baccalaureate, master's, certificates of advanced study, and doctoral levels. The doctoral program was initiated in recent years. More than 500 master's degrees were awarded in 1985 together with 350 baccalaureate degrees. Grants exceeding $600,000 were received in 1985, principally from local school systems. Programs of study include early childhood, elementary and special education, school psychology, computer education, curriculum and instruction, reading, instructional leadership, and mathematics and science education.

College B is part of a comprehensive state university in the Midwest. Its eighty-three full-time education faculty serve 1,500 full-time-equivalent students at the baccalaureate, masters, certificate of advanced study, and doctoral levels. More than 170 undergraduate, 144 masters, and forty-four doctoral degrees were awarded in 1985. The college received approximately $505,000 in grant funds in 1985. Education programs of study include early childhood, elementary, secondary, special education, educational administration, school psychology, counselor education, and educational foundations.

College C is a private institution in the Northeast. Of the ninety-seven full-time faculty, twenty-three are in the education division. Undergraduate education enrollments exceed 300, virtually all of whom are full-time. Graduate education enrollment (master's level) numbers approximately 500, most of whom are full-time. The education division has one externally funded grant. Degree programs exist in elementary, secondary, special, art and music education, and in communication disorders.

Examination of Table III shows that the differences in mission are somewhat reflected in the percentages. The two institutions with doctoral responsibilities show greater time allocated to scholarship. That faculty in College B, with an established doctoral program, report less time on scholarship than College A with a new doctoral program is an intriguing finding.

The absence of any reported practicum supervision responsibilities on the part of the faculty from College C was puzzling, given that college's missions. Subsequent discussion with an administrator revealed that clinical supervision of students was performed by faculty with part-time appointments. The use of part-time faculty in this instance reinforces the caveat that sample size and this study's dependence on volunteer respondents must be continually considered.

The greater amount of time spent by College C faculty on instruction than at Colleges A and B is explainable, perhaps, on the basis of activities directed by the latter two toward external grant responsibilities. On the other hand, the average scheduled class instructional assignment for College C is only marginally higher (7.8) than for College A (6.8). While the instructional load for College C is a third higher than College B, the nearly 50 percent greater effort in instruction, especially in the absence of any practicum supervision, suggests the work ethos in each institution.

It is difficult to interpret the differences in aggregate service shown because of the small amounts of time allocated to such activity. The substantial differences, however, among the colleges in faculty time allocated to administration and governance require less caution. Faculty in College B clearly spend substantially greater proportions of their time on such matters. The reasons for this difference are not clear.

Further analysis revealed some striking differences in respect to scholarly activities, confirming opinions widely held within the teacher education professoriate. Comparisons were made between each faculty member's ranked position in the *Instruction* category with where that same faculty member is positioned in the *Scholarship* category. Of the thirteen faculty displaying the highest allocations to instruction, only four are similarly ranked for time allocated to scholarship. The high thirteen on scholarship allocated an aggregate 258 hours to scholarship and 203 hours to instruction; the low fourteen allocated 46 hours to scholarship but 398 to instruction. The generalization that those who devote their energies to instruction spend less time on scholarship is supported by these data.

Similar comparisons may be drawn between other activities. The relationship of the top ranked faculty on advising relative to their position for scholarship is equally as great in a negative direction as the distinction between instruction and scholarship; nine of the high thirteen on advising were among the lower one-half in scholarship.

On the other hand, those who ranked in the upper one-half on advising time are disproportionately found among the high allocators in instruction and administration/governance. In both instances, eight out of thirteen shared their positions in the upper one-half. This may be indicative of a service or person-directed orientation generic to all three kinds of activities.

## METHODOLOGICAL CAUTIONS

Extrapolating these findings to other campuses would be difficult. Many mitigating factors may have entered into the distribution of time to activity categories for individual faculty. These include: (1) respondents were volunteers and willing to undertake a nuisance task for a solid week (see Author's Note 1); (2) the time of the year the logs were kept (May), perhaps leading to underemphasis on preparation and overemphasis of evaluation of student work and ceremonial functions; (3) not knowing whether faculty were long-tenured, mid-career, or beginning professors; and (4) neglecting to ask each faculty member for his or her work assignment for the quarter to stand as a template against which time allocations might be better understood.

Distortion of campus results may exist as a result of sampling problems. Faculty in College B were volunteers from the ranks of those awarded merit pay the preceding year. Faculty from College C were adjudged to be a good cross-section by the administrator who facilitated the collection of the logs. Faculty from College A were seen as a "cut above the average" by their facilitating administrator.

Possible mistakes in coding entries are another concern. Another may exist in the rather astounding discovery that out of a total of 92,721 professional minutes logged by these twenty-seven faculty, only 275 were allocated to general professional reading or discursive journal reading. Perhaps more of such activity did take place. If it did, it was identified in a fashion that obscured its nature. Finally, the decision to consider doctoral committee/dissertation responsibilities as part of "scholarship" may artificially inflate the investment in inquiry-related activities.

Maintaining confidentiality precluded being able to ask respondents questions about workload. For how many classes, with how many students, of what credit hour value were the respondents responsible? For how many student teachers or other practicum assignments were they responsible? Was any time released on a grant? Were scheduled office hours kept? How many hours? Did respondents hold governance or administrative responsibilities and of what kind? Did they have formal responsibilities and of what kind? Did they have formal responsibilities related to their profession beyond their institutional assignments? This kind of information would have afforded additional insights into the time allocations reported.

## DISCUSSION

While there are many reasons for being cautious about the data, the raw tabulation of self-reported time in this pilot study is revealing. The allocation of individual faculty effort varies far beyond what would be expected by individual assignments. Table II illustrates that variation in terms of range. The high/middle/low analyses in Table III display another dimension of that variation. Some individuals and groups of faculty demonstrate differences in investment of their time to key activities that actually constitute multiples of that invested by others. For example, the faculty member spending the most total professional time in the recorded week devoted more than twice as much as the faculty member spending the least. The popular image of the faculty member as a type, implying a set of activities all perform, is seriously challenged by these data. Of these twenty-seven faculty, only two activities were performed by all: (1) preparation for a current or future teaching assignment, and (2) administrative chores. In any given week, differences in assignment coupled with the autonomy individual faculty enjoy in defining their work, produce the dramatic variations recorded.

If the mass of teacher educators hold a set of norms and values, it does not appear to have a common shaping effect. Clearly, differences exist across the campuses on the way faculty spend their time. Some of those differences may be explained by institutional mission. For example, one would expect proportionally more scholarship in colleges with doctoral responsibilities. On the other hand, should the faculty in professional training programs differ as much as reported here in the amount of service time recorded? Should not all professional training programs be staffed by faculty who allocate at least a significant portion of their time to scholarship? Perhaps the most dramatic interinstitutional difference is the amount of administration/ governance time invested by faculty in College B. That College B is a great variance with Colleges A and C is apparent and worth more detailed consideration by anyone at College B interested in increasing time investments to other functions.

Widely held opinions about the inverse relationship that exists among heavy teachers and heavy scholars and, for that matter, between scholarship in relation to advising, service, and administration are borne out by the data. The way individual faculty define their teaching and advising responsibilities has important meaning for the amount of time available for scholarship.

While the average amount of time spent by faculty on scholarship is about one-fifth of their working week, a relatively small group of high performers is responsible for that average. In fact, only ten of the twenty-seven allocate time to scholarship at above the "average"; the remaining seventeen invest, on the average, only slightly more than four hours a week to scholarship.

Part of the impetus for this study was a desire to understand the ethos of colleges of education that supports or inhibits scholarship. These data illustrate the press of other functions on professorial life. The seventeen faculty below the mean for scholarship report nearly fifty-six hour work week, close to the overall average of time spent by the total group. It is not realistic to suggest an "additional commitment" as a strategy to increase the amount of time devoted to scholarship by this group. On the other hand, the ten faculty above the mean find time for scholarship. These persons are from the two colleges with doctoral programs, but these ten respondents seem not to be prevented by their other responsibilities from investing time in scholarship.

Finally, if faculty members develop the patterns and skills of discursive or general professional reading during their graduate study, this evidence suggests the use of those skills does not continue into their professorships. Finding only 275 minutes devoted to general professional reading out of a total of 92,271 minutes was a major surprise. It may mean only that faculty see such reading as associated with class preparation, their scholarly writing, or the activities lumped under administration. It may be that such reading is not done during the teaching quarter, but during breaks and summers.

## RECOMMENDATIONS

A concern that the culture of teacher education does not adequately support scholarly activities was the undergirding reason for this pilot study. The data collected, although limited, are actually rather positive. If the norms and attitudes within teacher education are unsupportive of scholarship, the variations among three campuses suggest that institutional norms may be more powerful than individual professional norms. While institutional norms are not easy to alter, the task is far easier than shifting amorphous professional norms as they are internalized for each individual. Institutional variations suggest that individual professors are not "locked-in" by the existence of broader norms antagonistic or unsupportive of scholarship activity. It is also clear that within institutions, much needs to be done to increase the time and attention to scholarship among teacher educators. Based on the data in the logs, the following suggestions may be worthy of consideration by those responsible for teacher education:

A. The technique of keeping faculty logs is a promising practice from both individual and institutional perspectives. Individual faculty members might use the technique to acquire a data-based sense of congruence with personal intent. Individual faculty might adjust their work to achieve congruence with desires that may differ from the reality revealed.

Institutions may employ the technique as a stimulus to faculty development activities or as evidence in support for resource requests. If a college undertakes the exercise, experience suggests the importance of: (1) anonymity; (2) clarity and openness about the purposes and uses of the data: and (3) recognition of the time demands on both the keepers of the logs and those who will perform the analysis.

It is strongly recommended that basic, tabular data be the vehicle for unit consideration. This technique preserves anonymity and focuses attention on the unit, on the ethos of the college. Once the data are considered, faculty and administration will be in a stronger position to address curricula, productivity, work load, and resource questions.

B. Data in the faculty logs suggest the application of this simple technique might direct faculty attention to scholarship. The logs also may reinforce the finding that two faculty functions are served without fail: meeting classes and keeping office hours. Teaching and advising are clearly high priorities. If scholarship is to be enhanced, some changes must be considered beyond the normal reward structure. For example, a college might specify that every faculty member had the privilege of defining a four-hour block of time for scholarship. Once chosen, that block of time could not be interfered with by a dean, department head, or governance committees. No dean or department head would schedule a conference during a faculty member's instructional time or office hours. In essence, the four-hour scholarship block would be as inviolate as a scheduled class. This approach would strongly communicate that scholarship has equal priority with teaching, advising, and field activities.

C. A final suggestion grows out of the extremely small amount of time reported devoted to journal reading. More reading might have been buried under time allocated to class preparation, research, or writing. Experience raises doubts about this possible explanation. The place to address this concern may be in doctoral programs when students are socialized to the norms of the academy. If students are expected to adopt behaviors they will carry with them into their careers, professors need to be far more explicit about the critical importance of keeping abreast of developments in one's field.

The lack of emphasis on journal reading in doctoral programs was discerned when the writer asked several well-read faculty how they learned that journal reading was an important part of their responsibilities. Most recollect no attention to such matters in their graduate study. Most claim to have developed their own approaches, some of which were highly personalized. Many admit that they look at journals because they write, not the other way around. The motivation, some admitted frankly, is, in part, self- interest; one cannot afford to try to publish material ignorant of relevant developments already published. Virtually all acknowledged that "keeping up" was one of the most important moral obligations of professorial life.

What was especially intriguing about these conversations about journal reading was the way they spilled over into other issues about socialization to the professorial role: the way one learned about which organizations to join; what joining them meant; how attendance at annual meetings is related to literature in the field; what to—and not to—expect at annual meetings; how one learns the ropes of bringing one's ideas to the attention of others in the professional academy, including but not restricted to publishing; and so on. Curiously, in these conversations the quick movement from "reading journals" to topics like these confirms the assessment that such behavior is part of the culture of academe. This observation is a confirmation, in turn, of the sense that whether it occurs is intimately connected to the ethos in any given institution.


## CONCLUSION

This pilot project demonstrated the extent of the demands that involvement in such a study makes on all its participants. It is no wonder that so little is known about the way persons actually spend their time. The self-reported nature of the data is an obvious concern. Still, much was learned. The primary purpose of the activity was to stimulate thinking about the realities and puzzles of undertaking scholarship in teacher education units.

Attention to such matters ought to be encouraged. Hopefully, others will undertake similar studies designed to engage faculty and administrator attention on questions that probe a college's ethos. Such inquiries should be periodically repeated. They might well encourage reflection and scholarship throughout teacher education.

## REFERENCES

Tucker, S. B. (1984). Increasing the research capacity of schools of education: A policy inquiry, March 1981. In H. Gideonse & E. Joseph (Eds.), *Increasing research capacity in schools of education: A policy inquiry and dialogue* (pp. 7– 28). Cincinnati, Ohio: Fleuron Press.

Yuker, H. E. (1984). *Faculty workload: Research, theory, and interpretation.* (Report No. 10). Washington, D.C.: Association of the Study of Higher Education. (ERIC Document Reproduction Service No. *ED 259 691.*)

*Author's Note:*

1. Harold E. Yuker's (1984) comments about samples in studies of faculty workload are especially pertinent here: ". . . one should not assume that those who do not respond are similar to those who do" (p. 16).

# 9

# The Ideal Professor
# of Education

## RICHARD WISNIEWSKI

Early in our deliberations, our group engaged in an exercise in which we offered visions of the ideal professor:

Ducharme's ideal

> wonders if most people's careers are, in a sense, accidental. He speculates if anybody, sitting in a high school classroom dreaming away the hours of a late spring afternoon . . . ever thinks about becoming a professor of education. He decides that probably no one has ever had such a thought. He is mildly saddened by this realization.

Schwebel offered:

> The ideal professors wear no halos. They know they are capable of error and that they err. At the same time they are deeply committed to the belief that humans have an extraordinary capacity to transform weakness into strength . . . [that] they are

people in process of developing—in process of becoming the ideal professor.

Gideonse said:

My ideal professor of education would move [uncomfortably] back and forth between the worlds of theory and practice, mindful of the epistemological peculiarities of each along with the fundamentally different orientations.

Raths stated:

He has not lost his love of puzzlements and wonderments. He is disposed to read the research journals and related works that have to do with the philosophy and history of teacher education. His colleagues think of him as being especially well-informed. His strength lies, however, in how he uses his information.

The ritual of tenure, promotion, and merit decisions suggests another approach to defining the ideal professor. During the process, statements such as the following are often heard: "Which is more important, teaching, research, or professional service?" "If I am to emphasize research, my teaching load must be reduced." "I am active in professional service, working with the schools, and cannot be expected to engage in research." "The only thing that is rewarded in this college is publications." "Those of us committed to teaching in-service never get our share of the rewards." "There is much poor research published and I refuse to add to the mess." "People strong in research should not be expected to engage in service activities."

These illustrations make clear that many professors do not believe they should be expected to perform in all three areas of professorial responsibility. Nonetheless, the thesis here is that an ideal professor values and nurtures the interrelationships among scholarship, teaching, and professional service. Admittedly an exasperated view, perhaps the ideal professor is simply someone who does not have to be told this is the case.

Despite the interminable debate about the matter, a commitment to scholarship, the essence of university life, must characterize all who prepare teachers. Those among our ranks who do not share this commitment contribute to our second-class status in the academy. That our status, deserved or maligned, is the result of many factors does not alter the fundamental importance of scholarship in a university milieu. Until virtually all professors of education are practicing scholars, our status will not be improved.

## DEFINING THE IDEAL

Dictionaries define an ideal as a standard of perfection or a person or thing that embodies such a standard. No one can offer a precise definition of any ideal. Hence, the ideal proposed in this discussion is not made of granite. The appropriate analogy for the concept is electronic. A video screen on which a figure is suggested by dancing flashes of light is an illustration. The outline of the figure is clear, but shimmering; movement belies permanence; the image is at once distinct and then a part of other images. This comes close to embodying the dynamic type of ideal posited here.

It is recognized that proposing an ideal leads to "yes, but" reactions. Indeed, bemused interest may be the best response for which one can hope. There are compelling reasons to define the ideal professor, however. Questions regarding the quality of teacher education are voiced as never before. Such questions cannot be answered honestly without examining those who prepare teachers. An ideal provides a standard against which both norms and aspirations can be assessed.

Symbolic interactionist theory offers a framework for understanding any social role as well as for developing an ideal type. In essence, all who interact with professors set expectations for professorial behavior. In whose eyes is the ideal professor reflected? In the eyes of students? Of other professors? Of teachers, principals, and superintendents? Of college administrators? The ideal is an amalgam of all these perceptions, hence the shimmering, shifting definition suggested above. The expectations of many differing groups create the several types of professors found in schools of education.

Other writers have categorized professors of education into types. Jackson's typology includes disciplinists, generalists and pedagogists (Jackson, 1975). More recent writers have suggested similar categories. Roemer and Martinello (1982) identify disciplinists, technologists and those who apply the work of both. Finkelstein (1982) offers another tripate division: technicians, mandarins, and witnesses. Most recently, Ducharme and Agne (1987) describe educationists as beasts of burden, facilitators, and academicians. Similarities and differences among these types reveal that deep schisms divide education faculties. All of these categorizations are revealing and useful.

The ideal suggested here incorporates the best of these sub-types. The ideal professor is what all professors of education should be like. Yet, other types exist and offer needed services. A professional school needs more than one type to fulfill its missions. At issue is the balance between various types, which is not static. It is reasonable to suggest, therefore, a shift in norms to where the proposed ideal would characterize most education faculties.

Of all the qualities needed, a commitment to a life of the mind is essential to being a professor. While a variety of tasks must be done in a college, the common denominator must be participation in the world of scholarship. Nelson (1981) quotes from a Davidson College faculty handbook statement which is illustrative of this view:

> Ideally the college professor would be a widely respected scholar excited about learning and capable of communicating this excitement to others, a teacher deeply concerned with the welfare of students and eager to have them learn and grow, one who teaches imaginatively both by books and by personal example, a demanding yet compassionate person who respects the moral worth of students and their potential for growth. While no one teacher is likely to realize all these attributes, the College must continually seek to recruit men and women who strive to do so to the greatest possible extent.

The key element is the phrase "a widely respected scholar." This discussion rests on this fundamental premise of academic life, with scholarship defined as all forms of creative and intellectual productivity.

Professors vary in their commitment to scholarship as they do in respect to teaching and other activities. Each of us stamps our personal characteristics, intellectual, emotional, and physical, on the behaviors embedded in the roles we play. Thinking of the professors with whom we studied or worked, we remember characteristics unique to individuals; for example, kindness, patience, and empathy, and their obverse traits. Even an ideal professor can sometimes be boring or mean-spirited. An intriguing aspect of such sociopsychological attributes is a professor's self-perception of his or her role. How does an awareness of self on a faculty determine one's behavior? Does one hide one's talents in an untalented group? Does one bloom in a group whose members have endowments superior to one's own? Or does one lord it over others in the first example and withdraw in the second?

Whatever the precise definition of an ideal type, comparisons between education professors and colleagues in liberal arts or other colleges introduce another intriguing variable, as suggested in Burch's chapter. The status of education professors is derived from such comparisons, and readers of this volume are probably knowledgeable of some contrasts. Just as some test means for education students have too often been in the lower half of university populations, the reputation of education professors is sometimes in the same category. This perception obscures two factors. First, many excellent students and professors are found in the education field, and comparisons are not always made by fair-minded individuals. In their exceptionally insightful analysis of colleges of education, Lopez and Balzer (1984) put it bluntly: "Part of the reputation is unadulterated prejudice" (p. 318). Second, most comparisons do not take into account the three or more subtypes of professors in a typical school of education.

## FACTORS DETERMINING PROFESSORIAL TYPES

At least three determinants of behavior in schools of education appear to be critical in explaining various professorial types: (1) the influence of prior school experience; (2) the nature of doctoral training for the professoriate; and, (3) the professors with whom one works in a given college.

As Ducharme and Agne discussed earlier, most education professors served in public schools for five or more years prior to earning a doctorate and joining a faculty. The values and behaviors of public schools and of the academy are at once parallel and divergent. Schoolteachers are surrounded by youth all day and must be "on" every professional hour. Professors teach a limited number of hours, with time to prepare for classes, to consult with students, to engage in scholarship, and to partially define their work. The success of teachers is almost exclusively defined in terms of classroom behavior. The university requires participation in the world of scholarship and research. The success of professors is ideally defined by the quality of mind brought to tasks, by the depth of knowledge generated by scholarship, and by the ideas professed.

To what degree do professors of education, conditioned by years in the public schools, adapt to the intellectual norms of university life? Ducharme and Agne argue that school experiences have an enduring impact on the lives of professors. Some professors make the transition to the academy successfully. Lopez and Balzar (1984) argue that most do not. Most education professors do not acknowledge that being a student of one's field is more important than merely meeting classes, no matter how skillful the teaching style.

With regard to training for the professoriate, the central point is that such training is almost always in another college of education. That the rigor of training influences future behaviors is hardly debatable. If most education professors exhibit a relatively low level of scholarship, their doctoral training may be an explanatory factor. Because scholarly activity is posited as the key to the ideal professor, the importance of rigorous doctoral study cannot be overstated.

The third factor is the performance level of one's peers, that is, the norms of the work place. This is the most critical and complex variable. Gideonse's chapter shows how splintered professional daily life can be. The ethos of schools of education can be divided into ideational and materialistic components. The ideational component includes values, aspirations, attainments, and expectations associated with a professor's work. The material part refers to institutional arrangements for work, such as teaching loads, office hours, teaching and clinical facilities, instructional materials, and so on. The impact of these latter factors is well-established. The impact of the ideational components is only beginning to be recognized (Wisniewski, 1984). (See Author's Note 2.)

These three explanatory factors are reflected in the way professors address the traditional areas of professorial responsibility: teaching, professional service, and scholarship. All three expectations are important, but the critical caveat must be underscored: scholarship is the most important of the three.

## SCHOLARSHIP AND THE IDEAL PROFESSOR

It may appear puerile to state the importance of scholarship or to argue it is part of an ideal. There are professors who exemplify the ideal. Regretfully, there are many who do not. The ratio between the two groups determines the rigor of preparation in and reputation of colleges of education. The ratio obviously varies among institutions. Experience, discourse, and the limited literature on the matter suggest that the ideal professor posited here is not the norm in most colleges of education, save in specific departments or rare institutions. A first-rate college of education deserves that status only when exceptions to the scholarly ideal are in the minority rather than the norm. Without an ongoing commitment to scholarship, a professor's contributions are hollow. Unless the overwhelming majority of professors in a college engage in scholarship, the institution's effectiveness is shallow.

The professor must be an authority with the ability to put theory into practice in professional settings. Teaching and service derive from the fount of scholarship. The ideal professor is a student throughout life, generating knowledge or critiques of knowledge produced by others. The ideal professor constantly searches and probes, questions conventional wisdom and established practices. The professor is intrigued with puzzle solving. These are intellectual activities, engaged in by persons comfortable with ideas, books, and all the trappings of the reflective life.

It is difficult for professors in any discipline to be reflective and scholarly in the American university. Faculty are consumed by the structured, bureaucratic procedures of modern university life. The relentless press of calendars, schedules, governance procedures, and a host of other factors do not foster scholarly reflection; they inhibit it. Despite these factors, the scholarly tradition, a spirit of inquiry, still characterizes many disciplines.

Colleges of education, however, are rarely centers of intellectual ferment. The relentless forces of segmentation and time constraints appear to have their strongest effects on schools of education, again perhaps because of the prior experience of so many professors in the schools. Interestingly, other professional schools suffer some of the same low scholarship norms as education. As Ducharme and Agne (1982) and Esch (1983) suggest, there is even evidence that colleges of education are no worse than some disciplines in respect to scholarly publication, but there is hardly unanimity on the matter. Disagreement on this or any assessment of preparation institutions is inevitable because there are so many of them. While some colleges of education encourage the intellectual milieu vital to scholarship, others are part of institutions where scholarship is neither expected nor rewarded.

The importance of teaching is one of the commonly held values among education professors. There is little agreement, however, on scholarship as the *sine qua non* of good teaching. It is the commitment to ongoing study that should qualify the professor to be a teacher. Yet, the range of teaching behaviors exhibited by professors is well-known. Students experience outstanding professors, some of whom are not scholars; they also tolerate terrible professors who may be scholars. These extremes only divert a focus on the ideal characteristic of a college teacher: a person immersed in a field of knowledge. How that person imparts/requires/encourages/limits access to knowledge and skills will vary, as will the person's teaching effectiveness because of personalistic variables and preparation for teaching. The essential common denominator is one's knowledge of a field. In order to be knowledgeable, the ideal professor reads and studies throughout his or her career. In a school of education, the scholar brings a probing and analytical mind to all questions associated with teaching and learning.

Granted, coasting on dated knowledge or on tricks of the trade can carry any reasonably intelligent person through the teaching act. This fact does not weaken the argument; it only reveals the tolerance accorded to teaching behaviors. Teaching is a public act; the setting is usually a classroom; and it is always performed before an audience. Students are subservient to the professor and a range of behaviors are tolerated. Personality variables rather than intellectual/scholarly norms are often utilized to explain variations in quality.

If colleges were saturated by professors who are active students of their craft, the reputation of education departments would be much stronger. The ideal college of education would be the most innovative and strongest teaching unit on campus, a reputation demonstrated by student evaluations and other forms of assessment. Such colleges would be widely acknowledged as centers of inquiry and practice related to teaching and learning. To some degree, some colleges now have such reputations. It is the level of intensity at which professors pursue the scholarly ideal that is the issue, not the fact that by tradition they are assumed to be experts in educational research by persons outside the profession. Is the commitment to research so clear, so broadly based, that there is no question regarding the matter? Few students of the professoriate can answer this question without qualification.

Professional service must also be predicated on ongoing scholarship. The professor providing counsel to practicing professionals should be disseminating state-of-the-art knowledge. As in teaching, professional service is at its best when performed by a highly knowledgeable person who has the additional talent of working well with people in the field.

In this connection, several states have mandated that professors of education periodically demonstrate ways by which they maintain contact with the field. These states require professors to return to school classrooms for limited periods of time. The fact that such legislation has been enacted reflects the perception that education faculty are distant from the schools for which they prepare practitioners. Ironically, it reflects the view of some outside academy that professors are too theoretical, too scholarly!

The ideal professor of education is not distant from the practicing profession. A normal part of the ideal professor's week regularly would be spent in schools. Like the ideal physician, the ideal professor maintains weekly rounds as part of his or her work. Just as some physicians visit hospitals with which they are associated, the ideal professor makes similar visits to schools. The visit might be in connection with mentoring an intern, with a special project, or other services for teachers or students. This expectation should apply to all professors of education with no distinction regarding the area of specialty. The equivalent of one full day each week would be the minimal expectation for this type of activity. The professor's visits to schools should be routine rather than exceptional events. Happily, some professors are already demonstrating this commitment. When every professor is engaged in such field work, it will weaken the perception, erroneous for fine professors, that educators do not care about, have escaped from, and are ignorant of the true conditions of teaching.

## ADDITIONAL CHARACTERISTICS OF THE IDEAL

There are additional characteristics of the ideal that go beyond the triumvirate of scholarship, teaching, and service. The temptation is to provide a long list but only two are underscored here: (1) expectations for student performance; and (2) a vigorous, visible commitment to public education. Ideal professors of education have high expectations of their students. They expect their students to demonstrate a commitment to learning and skill development that goes beyond the often routine expectations of courses. In respect to readings, papers, and other assignments, performance norms and grades reflect high expectations.

Grades in education have traditionally been above university norms. Whether student achievement levels warrant the high proportion of "As" awarded is an open question. That universities as a whole have "caught-up" with education in the grade inflation race begs the issue. Why did colleges of education lead in this phenomenon for decades? While institutional variations exist, why is it that education majors have historically been below the mean for other college students on ACT and SAT tests, yet earn higher grades? Happily, growing evidence indicates that education students are no longer below campus means (Applied Systems, 1985). If persons are ill-prepared for college work, the problem is now recognized as a campus-wide concern. And, of course, outstanding students are found in every program, including education. The legacy of past practices, however, has yet to be overcome.

Many professors are adept at rationalizing these questions but their explanations are not persuasive. Regretfully, colleges of education have earned reputations associated with low expectations of students. Professors with high expectations suffer from this image as much as those who nurture it. The fact that professors in any discipline will debate definitions of high achievement does not diminish the need for education professors to set high expectations of performance.

The final characteristic is a commitment to public education. A professor's role includes that of asking questions, and public education is not immune to criticism. Indeed, the schools need loving critics. In public institutions of teacher education, a commitment to public education, its improvement and preservation, is not debatable. It ought to be the one article of faith unique to the educational professoriate. Schwebel makes clear how difficult such a commitment is to fulfill. Nonetheless, in word and deed, the ideal professor of education in a public institution must demonstrate a deep commitment to public education. To do less is hypocrisy.

## CONCLUSION

With all the calls for education reform, professors who meet these ideals are more important than ever before in the history of teacher education. There is a tremendous need for scholarship on all facets of the changes being implemented in schools as well as in colleges of education. The opportunities to conduct scholarship, to provide professional service, and to examine one's own teaching in light of new research have never been greater. Professors of education are in a unique position to capitalize on these events. Despite the fears of many, this is an auspicious time for schools of education. Professors not actively engaged in renewing their storehouse of knowledge are missing a great opportunity; they continue to besmirch the reputation of their colleges.

Professors who have not engaged in scholarship since completing their dissertation cannot meet the ideal. Their lack of scholarly activity leads to a continued diminution of colleges of education.

Professors engaged in professional service who are divorced from scholarship appropriate to such service are skirting professional malfeasance. Professors who teach courses without regularly assessing the quality of their teaching mock the essence of the title *professor* of education. Being a student of the teaching/learning act is at the core of professing in a school of education.

Stating these and other convictions dogmatically is one way to underscore their importance. Applying them in departmental tenure, promotion, and merit decisions is difficult; but hard decisions cannot be avoided if norms are to be altered in a given setting. With regard to anticipated "yes, but" responses to the position expressed here, it is clear that rationalizations for the status quo are more powerful than any plea for ideal behaviors. At the same time, not stating this position, not attempting to define an ideal, is unacceptable, at least to those who believe colleges of education have the potential to be among the most innovative and intellectually stimulating departments on any campus.

And that is the point of this essay: Is one satisfied with one's station or is one determined to improve it? This writer desires to associate only with professors who are active in their field; with persons committed to strengthening their teaching, to probing and expanding their scholarship, to working closely with public schools; with professors who share the excitement of experimentation in education; and with professors from whom one can learn as a peer or as a student.

The ideal professor of education is one who values and takes pride in the interrelationship among scholarship, teaching and professional service. Such professors recognize that these activities nurture one another and cannot be separated. The ideal professor models behavior appropriate to these values and expects colleagues and students to behave similarly. The quality and reputation of colleges of education are largely determined by the degree to which we encourage this ideal in one another. When we do so, we live in the world described by Highet (1976):

> . . . Ours is a lively world, ringing with conflicts and buzzing with problems. One of the central principles governing both our teaching and our learning is incessant renewal. After a long career of strife and accomplishment, the first great Athenian, Solon, said that his last years were governed by the rule:
> I grow old learning much and always learning (p. 74).

REFERENCES

Applied Systems Institute, Inc. (1985). *Tomorrow's teachers* (rev. ed.). Washington, D.C.: U. S. Department of Education.

Ducharme, E. R., & Agne, R. M. (1982). The education professoriate: A research-based perspective. *Journal of Teacher Education, 33* (6), 36.

_____ (1987). Professors of education: Beasts of burden, facilitators, or academicians. *Journal of Human Behavior and Learning, 4,* 1–9.

Esch, M. (1983). Education research productivity of institutions of higher education. *American Educational Research Journal, 20* (Spring), 6.

Finkelstein, B. (1982). Technicians, mandarins, and witnesses: Searching for professional understanding. *Journal of Teacher Education, 33* (3), 25–27.

Gideonse, H., & Joseph, E. (1984). *Increasing research capacity in schools of education: A policy inquiry and dialogue.* Cincinnati, Ohio: Fleuron Press.

Highet, G. (1976). *The immortal profession: The joys of teaching and learning.* New York: Weybright and Talley.

Jackson, P. W. (1975). Divided we stand: Observations on the internal organization of the education professoriate. In A. Bagley (Ed.), *The professor of education: An assessment of conditions* (pp. 61–70). Minneapolis: Society of Professors of Education, College of Education, University of Minnesota.

Lopez, T. R., & Balzar, D. M. (1984). Possibilities for the scholarly life in colleges of education. In D. Tavel (Ed.), *Modern educational controversies* (p. 318). Lanham, Md.: University of America Press.

Nelson, W. C., (1981). *Renewal of the teacher-scholar: faculty development in the liberal arts college* (p. 7). Washington, D.C.: Association of American Colleges.

Roemer, R. E., & Martinello, M. L. & Martinello, M. L. (1982). Divisions in the education professoriate and the future of professional education. *Educational Studies, 13* (Summer), 203–23.

Wisniewski, R. (1984). The scholarly ethos in schools of education. *Journal of Teacher Education, 35* (5), 2–8.

*Author's Notes:*

1. A shortened version of this chapter was published in the *Phi Delta Kappan*, 1986, *68* (4), 288–92. Adapted with permission; copyright 1986, Phi Delta Kappan.

2. For an analysis of an effort to engage deans of education in dialogue on the importance of inquiry and scholarship, see H. Gideonse and E. Joseph (1984).

# 10

# Where We Stand

RICHARD WISNIEWSKI
EDWARD R. DUCHARME

We have analyzed the professors of teaching, their characteristics, productivity, and status. We have touched on the world of teaching and its relationship to schools of education. We have posited an ideal for the education professoriate. As in the tendency in such discussions, we sometimes dwelled on problems rather than on positive attributes. There are also strengths in our calling and our hopes for the future are based on the presence of many excellent professors of education.

Historically, functionally, and legally, the education professoriate is secure within the academic firmament. The preparation of teachers is as vital to society's prepetuation as any other professional preparation program. Schools, colleges, and departments of education are as much a part of the campus scene as departments of history, chemistry, or other disciplines. While their position within the academic pecking order is often questioned, professors of education enjoy all the privileges and opportunities of the academic community. Education is hardly a minor profession. Despite decades of both legitimate and unfounded criticism, the education professoriate has survived and thrived.

Education is a mass and uneven enterprise, however, and criticisms of public schools attach to colleges of education. Educationists are unique from other professors in that they are held directly accountable for the performance of their graduates. The relationship between a person's training and work is only partially visible in other professions. This is not the case for professors of education. Teachers are always in the public eye. As a result, professors of education are likely to be blamed whenever the quality of teaching is found wanting. Unfortunately, they are seldom praised when exemplary teachers are cited.

Some extreme critics call for the closing of all education colleges. Rarely have such recommendations been given serious consideration. Unless major changes take place in the professoriate and the programs they offer, attacks will continue. Support for schools of education will erode unless perceptions of their professors are improved. Because our concern is with the quality of our profession, we believe some teacher preparation programs should be closed. We are speaking of colleges that have neither the resources nor the faculty and administrative commitments requisite to complying with increased expectations.

Because of such concerns, this chapter is specifically addressed to colleagues in the education professoriate. A sense of common purpose is our goal, but nothing is harder to attain. The professors of teaching are not a unified group and our division into educational specialties weakens our commitment to education writ large. Nonetheless, we plead for cohesiveness. Whether we be professors of educational psychology, curriculum, or adult education, our allegiance must be to our roots: the preparation of teachers. This conviction is our fundamental premise as we offer our hopes for the future. We ask the commitment of our colleagues:

1. to the education of teachers as a fundamental purpose of the education professoriate. Unless the overwhelming bulk of professors place the preparation of teachers first in their commitments, and their area of specialization second, the fragmentation that now characterizes schools of education will persist;
2. to the generation and utilization of scholarship on a scale far beyond the norms in many schools of education at present; and,
3. to a new relationship with the practicing profession, one that encourages and values collaboration in strengthening and preserving public education.

If most professors of education shared these beliefs, the professoriate would be a critical and creative force for change in America's schools. This is not our reputation or stance. Is it possible to develop a shared vision in the coming decades? We believe it already exists in small pockets and that is can grow; but it must be nurtured in every possible context.

To achieve these goals, we believe new forms of organization are needed; the current fragmented, departmentalized schools of education must be altered. We also believe that we have too many schools of education. We cannot achieve the quality needed as long as more are added and few are closed. Finally, we examine the debate regarding the length of teacher preparation. Within this heated issue, both the problems and potential of teacher education are revealed.

## THE PURPOSE OF THE PROFESSORIATE

Hazlett may be right in asserting that we have no history or shared vision or purpose. Allison's biographies confirm the mixed expectations that have been placed on professors of education from their earliest days. Nonetheless, we have traditions, values, and ideals. Our traditions lie in a commitment to teachers and schooling; our values are those that inhere in the scholarly, pedagogical, and service responsibilities of the academy. Our ideals are embodied in faith in the power of education for human and social improvement. The centrality of teachers and of schools to this society establishes and enhances our legitimacy in academe.

The study of teaching and learning and the preparation of teachers are our *raisons d'etre*. Preparation programs for other professional roles—principals, counselors, social workers, or librarians—are important but subsidiary to the prime task of preparing teachers. It is in the preparation of teachers that we fulfill or fail in our mission. Teachers and teaching are the foundation from which all other educational roles derive.

We have responsibility for knowledge generation and dissemination. We must contribute to, remain abreast of, show the application of, and promote fidelity to pedagogical scholarship. Our knowledge base is becoming increasingly sophisticated and reliable. It is central to standards for professional recruitment, preparation, graduation, certification, employment, and continuing education It must permeate our professional work as never before. The coming decade will provide volatile arenas for the testing of our knowledge base.

## SCHOLARSHIP AND RESEARCH

Scholarship is the *sine qua non* of the professorial life, a fact evaded by a significant number of our colleagues. For generations many of our predecessors lived academic half-lives, neither producers nor consumers of scholarship. Intensely pragmatic and practitioner-oriented, they eschewed and downplayed the importance of scholarly inquiry. Such attitudes were perhaps acceptable in an earlier time. In the 1980s and beyond, such attitudes and behaviors are totally unacceptable.

We must not lose the warmth and compassion that emanated from education faculty a generation ago; we must however challenge programs where conventional wisdom, mythology, guesswork, and pragmatism were and are accepted as a knowledge base. The past of the education professoriate is not unlike that in medical schools, before the research era burst upon that field. Many in the education professoriate obtained their introduction to the profession from kindly, well-disposed faculty who wanted the best for their students and for those whom they, in turn, would teach. Often, their approach was personal and warm but scarcely intellectual. The humane qualities of that earlier era must be augmented with a penchant for inquiry, a bent for scholarship, and a critical turn of mind toward emerging knowledge.

We are aware that there is much more to be learned about teaching. We lament the fact, however, that what is known is not widely integrated into curricula. While we respect the attitudes and beliefs of an earlier generation, we stand unequivocally in favor or professional practice based on sound scholarship. Anything less in appointing, tenuring, or promoting professors reduces colleges of education to a trade school mentality.

As we write this, we are cognizant of Sizer and Powell's (1969) view:

> . . . The questioning and analysis which are at the heart of any soul who has had the audacity to 'profess' is still rare in the profession; and the profession must face this fact squarely. We talk of new recruits, new models. They are to be found; but they are still in small numbers compared with the need. The unreflective, unquestioning (if frighteningly well-meaning) professor is still, alas, the rule. May his tribe decrease.

We believe the tribe has decreased, but the condition described, twenty years later, still is the norm. What will be the assessment twenty years hence?

## RELATIONSHIP TO THE FIELD

The future of schools and colleges of education is inextricably linked with the public schools. The Holmes and Carnegie reports contend that cooperation and collaboration with the schools are necessary for reform. We agree.

*Collaboration* is a much used and abused word. Unexamined, it suggests that whatever tasks are to be done can be done equally by all participants. It has often been a catch-word for education professors bringing their ideas to schools and telling teachers what to do. We mean neither an unthinking acceptance of the view that all partners in an activity are equally fit to do all things, nor an elitist view that one group has wisdom and experience superior to the other. We posit an ideal yet to be realized: collaboration that capitalizes on the research and knowledge of the best professors in the academy and on the expertise and experience of the best teachers in the schools, recognizing that valuable attributes reside in both places. The proposed designation of selected schools as Professional Development Centers has the potential to unite outstanding teachers with exemplary professors for staff development, curriculum work, internship supervision, mentoring, and other matters.

The fact that the signature of the chief academic officer is necessary for membership in the Holmes Group offers a clue to the future. It suggests the possibility of a strengthened institutional commitment to education schools working with schools as part of their academic responsibility, perhaps even affecting the reward structure of higher education. This view is reinforced by a 1987 statement signed by thirty-seven university presidents. (Chronicle, 1987). In a document circulated to higher education institutions nationally, these presidents called for a renewed dedication to the improvement of public education and the teaching profession.

The blending of two social systems—the schools and higher education units—is difficult. Each system has its own reward structures and behavior patterns. Past failures to fuse the two social systems suggest the enormity of the task. We urge a renewed commitment to this work in the belief that, given current needs and demands, the increase in useful research, the national interest in teaching, success is more likely than in previous generations.

In order for successes to occur, changes in faculty attitudes and behaviors are requisite. Status in higher education helps to explain the social distance some professors maintain from the practicing profession. As Raths and his colleagues stress, the education professoriate exists in two cultures: the worlds of theory and practice. The professoriate's theory and knowledge generating functions are compatible with traditional academic practice, but its practical, field-oriented functions often lead to conflict or lowered status in the academy. Professors who "stray" from campus for too long may never find acceptance among their colleagues. Close linkages to the practicing profession are vital, yet they sometimes remove professors from the mainstream and rewards of academic life. All professional schools have a similar problem, but colleges of education have a particularly virulent form of the dilemma.

There is a way of overcoming the problem: field work combined with scholarship. They are not incompatible save to persons of limited talents. Combining the two is at the very heart of our calling. The opportunities for the enhancement of academic standing by conducting powerful research in schools are enormous. We may never do away with the notion that field work is of little value to the academic community, but field research leading to scholarly publication makes such work respected. We need only mention the concept of action research to suggest how long the problem and solution have been with us.

Some professors have learned to combine field work and scholarly efforts; others have been unable or unwilling to link their scholarship to the schools. The former are examples of the ideal professor described earlier. We are convinced that the education professoriate must serve both the academy and the schools. We urge a shift from a grudging acceptance of this dual responsibility to a spirited embrace of it. We must transform the world of teaching and learning. In order to do so, we must reside in the twin worlds of the academy and the public schools. Some faculty already do so; many more must. A number of states now mandate such relationships.

We cannot resolve the problems inherent in these situations, but we offer a point of view. The education professoriate, first and foremost, must be characterized by professors who are active producers and consumers of scholarship. There is no necessary cleavage between theory and practice. Those who separate them do a disservice to themselves, their colleagues, and their profession.

Some faculty are unlikely to contribute to scholarship; they will behave in the future as they have in the past. Such individuals are not conversant with the research literature; they perpetuate the stereotypical image of low intellectual quality in education courses. They increasingly are the few, rather than the norm on faculties. They are serving out their last years in the professoriate and are unlikely to alter their behaviors. We can do little more than admit their existence, work around them, and get on with the important work to be done.

There are professors solely committed to the world of practice who have never been socialized to the norms of the academy, but we see this group's control of programs and colleges diminishing. At the opposite end of the continuum of enculturation are professors extraordinarily active in scholarship but indifferent to the world of practice. The contributions of both types are needed, but both groups must recognize that their polar positions weaken the total enterprise. Reorganized and reconceptualized colleges and schools of education must fuse the actions, skills, and knowledge of these two groups in order to serve better the education of teachers and improve life in the schools.

We also ask ourselves if education units have the potential, in terms of the intellectual power of their faculties, to produce more scholarship. Certainly, units dominated by the type of faculty described in the preceding paragraphs do not have such intellectual resources. but we are aware of many education professors doing what must be done and doing it well. The *Handbook of Research on Teaching* and the *Encyclopedia of Educational Research* are prime examples of the breadth and depth of the work being produced.

## THE ORGANIZATION OF EDUCATION UNITS

Most schools of education must undergo dramatic reorganizations to meet future demands. We insist on more autonomy for education units, autonomy to control admissions, set standards, prescribe curricula, and build on the liberal arts preparation of students. Colleges of education must be more akin to law colleges, which also build on a liberal arts foundation. We are speaking here, of course, only to the structural relationship of a professional school to its university campus.

Most colleges include departments of elementary and secondary education, special education, counseling, and administration. This historic mimicking of the organizational patterns of the public schools has made schools of education impotent in an era of reform. Such patterns of organization contribute to the individual faculty members' comfort and sense of identity. They have strengthened our areas of specialization and given us identities as counselor educators, sociologists of education, reading specialists, and so on. As a result, the true professors of teaching have diminished in status within their own colleges. In many ways, large colleges of education reflect campuswide status and pecking orders. Those professors most committed to the teaching profession are often viewed as "nonacademic" or weak. As graduate programs have increased in status, teachers have rightly perceived a growing gap between the colleges from which they graduated and the practicing profession.

The departmentalized form of college organization does not promote the cohesiveness needed for the dynamic, interdisciplinary programs we envisage. While each of us has disciplinary roots we treasure, we recognize that specialization and departmentalization inhibit innovation and interactions among faculty. All too often, departments serve mainly to foster student and faculty isolation. This is as true within schools of education as it is in other colleges.

Matters are complicated by the fact that major schools of education are complex; their missions extend beyond the preparation of teachers. Some programs in such schools are far distant from teacher preparation. Human services, counseling psychology, home economics, or nursing programs are often part of a school of education. Programs preparing higher education personnel are common, as are specialties in areas such as recreation, dance, and public health. The "fit" of these programs with the central mission of a school of education may or may not be comfortable or even easily explained. The inclusion or absence of any program is a function of tradition, local conditions, resources, and a host of other factors. Matters were further complicated during the precipitous drop in education enrollments during the 1970s. Many schools of education developed or annexed programs only tangentially linked to the preparation of teachers.

Our plea, therefore, for interdisciplinary collaboration is confounded by a mosaic of organizational forms and missions. The integration of faculty efforts is very difficult to achieve in highly diverse units. That some programs outside of teacher preparation are strong and bring luster to a college is not at issue. Our concern here is with the central purpose of schools of education, and that is the preparation of teachers. All other missions derive from and should support this central focus.

The traditions, levels of expectation, and patterns of behaviors associated with schools of education are deeply entrenched, thereby making the achievement of innovative, scholarly schools of education difficult. We do not suggest an ideal organizational pattern for all education schools. There are simply too many differences in institutional cultures and histories that must be considered. Shafer's (1967) proposal to make schools centers of inquiry is one model for the type of colleges we envision.

In such colleges, interdisciplinary studies would be the norm rather than the exception. Teams composed of professors, clinical associates drawn from the ranks of outstanding practitioners, and advanced graduate students would teach and mentor cohorts of students. Such teams would demonstrate the skills and commitments of teaching needed by all teachers, exhibiting high standards of performance for themselves and their students. Gender and ethnic inequities would not be tolerated by such a faculty. The preparation of counselors and administrators would be predicated on the same assumptions and goals as those undergirding teacher preparation; the current segmentation of preparation for such roles would be viewed as a historical anamoly.

Inquiry, problem solving, and reflection would be among the behaviors most frequently exhibited by faculty and students alike in such a college. The blending of campus and practical applications in schools would be reflected in the daily schedules of all concerned. Individualized learning would be highly valued, but standards of achievement would not be compromised. However idealistic, it is on such concepts that professional schools of education should be structured. Other models may be posited, of course. These ideas merely suggest values we treasure.

While we strongly affirm the need for restructuring schools of education, we do not advocate a return to normal schools. Even increased autonomy for education schools does not mean a retreat from the university culture. We are opposed to any separation of schools of education from the university campus. Whatever the new forms of organization, the university must remain the setting for the preparation of teachers. The intellectual roots of teaching and learning are strongest on university campuses. Saying this in no way diminishes our commitment to collaboration with the practicing profession.

## THE NUMBER AND QUALITY OF SCHOOLS OF EDUCATION

Related to the organizational issue is the number of teacher preparation institutions in the nation. Our assessment of the talent pool in the professoriate, of scholarly productivity, and of the overall quality of the total enterprise leads us to the conclusion that the number of institutions preparing teachers must be reduced in the coming decades. Some public and private institutions cannot meet the demands for quality that permeate the reform literature. They simply do not have the faculty depth or resources for first-rate programs. Some purport to offer preparation programs with only one or two faculty members, for example. Preparing teachers on the cheap has been and remains one of our profession's dirty little secrets. Fewer than one-half of the institutions preparing teachers are accredited by the National Council for the Accreditation of Teacher Education. This fact is compelling evidence of the range in quality that now characterizes programs.

Even with reorganization and a reduction in numbers, a fundamental change in thinking is requisite. Gideonse (1987) has written of the need for a sense of clinical fidelity in schools of education, a concept demanding that the education professoriate exhibit the best practices of teaching in their own classrooms. Because the processes of teaching and learning form the essence of their discipline, professors of education by definition should and must be introspective about their own teaching. More than professors in any other discipline, they must explicitly profess and practice state-of-the-art pedagogical knowledge. To do less, as in the case of scholarship, only perpetuates mediocrity.

Major professional associations in which professors of education are active reflect emphases that will affect the organization and practice of education units on campus. A steady improvement in the quantity and quality of research by the education professoriate is evident at meetings of the American Education Research Association and similar groups. Analyses of recent issues of scholarly journals reveal a growing cadre of scholars making increasingly important contributions. An emerging cohort of young doctoral graduates starting promising intellectual careers also offers hope.

Annual meetings of the American Association of Colleges for Teacher Education now show evidence of carefully prepared and refereed presentations rather than programs dominated by the exchange of homilies. The Society of Professors of Education and similar groups regularly provide forums for scholarly debate. The Association of Teacher Educators, in their national meetings, has moved toward a focus on research and documentation rather than conventions highlighting inspirational speakers and "how-to" presentations. The redesign of standards by the National Council for the Accreditation of Teacher Preparation is another illustration of a growing recognition that increased rigor must be the hallmark of schools of education.

We believe that these trends, however uneven, indicate a discernible improvement in the quality and the respectability of the work of the education professoriate. The knowledge and skills manifested in these activities suggest that a critical mass of practicing scholars can effect educational reform as has no comparable group in the past.

The quality of doctoral graduates is also steadily rising. New faculty members do not appear to need the intense enculturation to academe that some of us needed twenty or more years ago when we began our careers. New appointees often come with a line of research already underway, with an expectation that they will succeed in teaching and simultaneously make a contribution to scholarship. New faculty frequently embarrass full professors in respect to scholarly productivity. Ducharme and Agne illustrate this point in their chapter.

While these signs are heartening, the composition of the education professoriate still reveals serious gender, racial and equity issues. The data from all sources reveal that much must be done to resolve these issues. If teacher education students are to value cultural diversity, they must experience such diversity. Faculties and administrators have the power to ensure that such diversity is present in their midst, however difficult the process.

While the education professoriate has not had many openings for new faculty, demographic data suggest a wave of retirements in the 1990s will provide an opportunity to appoint fresh scholars to the field. These conditions reinforce the need for reorganized schools of education. New types of interdisciplinary units will enable both new and experienced faculty to make maximum contributions to the profession.

## THE CONTROVERSY OVER THE "LENGTH" OF TEACHER PREPARATION

Throughout the 1980s, the debate about how long it takes to prepare a professional teacher has waxed with some fury. The professoriate is divided on the issue with respected colleagues taking differing views. Some advocate four years of liberal arts education followed by an intensive, professional year including an internship; others defend current practices. Others posit variants of the master of arts in teaching model. The Holmes and Carnegie proposals demand the end to the education baccalaureate. Yet even individuals within Holmes Group institutions question the wisdom of terminating four-year teacher education programs.

The controversy is far from resolution. The period of greatest heat about these issues coincided with the writing of this book. Would that the results of proposed options were as clear as their advocates suggest. Would that the abolishment of undergraduate teacher education have the salubrious results posited by the Holmes and Carnegie statements. Would that the emergence of professional development schools guarantee effective teachers at the end of the process; that "off the street" liberal arts graduates could, with minimal pedagogical preparation, function effectively in schools; or that proposed specialized roles for teachers could truly differentiate teacher performance. Would that all the solutions advocated by national commissions produce the results their advocates propose.

No one of the sometimes cross–purposed proposals can stand alone. Unfortunately, outside of anecdotes, war stories, and individual recollections, evidence is scant on many of these proposals. There are both effective and ineffective teachers from four-year programs of preparation; the same can be said of the graduates of liberal arts programs who subsequently became teachers. Unfortunately, we do not know enough empirically about large cohorts of teachers to state definitively the relationships between teaching performance and preparation, especially with respect to both content and length of preparation time.

There is much more to teaching than the number of credits in professional education or liberal arts. A more holistic understanding of the matter is emerging. The quality of preparation and the level of expectations for students preparing to teach are two keys to the puzzle, as are careful selection and admission procedures. Even more important are teaching conditions in schools. It is the work place that molds and controls the behaviors of teachers and students alike. Only in recent years has the impact of teaching conditions been recognized as the most powerful force determining teacher behaviors and effectiveness. Changes in campus preparation programs must be directly related to new forms of inducting teachers to new roles in schools. This realization is at the core of Carnegie, the Holmes Group, and other reform proposals.

We also support initiatives for strengthening the liberal arts background of all teachers. Teachers must be steeped in the very best that academic institutions can provide. Again, more liberal arts in and of itself is not *the* answer to problems in teacher education. The disarray in liberal arts regarding purposes, curricula, and the efficacy of undergraduate teaching is well-known. Nonetheless, the liberal arts are at the heart of the academy's goals of encouraging inquiry, questioning, and a sense of perspective. We respect the ideal of what a liberal arts education at its best can achieve, knowning full well the problems in achicving this goal.

A liberal education was critical in the personal and professional developments of all the contributors to this volume. We see the power of this type of background among our strongest students. We have seen too many persons with weak academic qualities pass through schools of education. Therefore, we urge support for programs requiring the liberal arts degree while demanding rigorous assessments of the graduates of such programs. What the education professoriate must guard against, as well as policymakers, is an uncritical acceptance of any proposed solution as *the* solution. Would that the conundrums of teacher preparation be so easily dispatched.

The question of how long it takes to prepare a teacher is only one key to strengthening the profession. Everything we know about human development, all that we have observed and experienced in schools, have taught us that competency and artistry in a complex arena of human interaction such as teaching are not time or program bound. While this is true of all professions, it apparently is difficult for some to see in the preparation of teachers.

Some graduates of schools of education, for many reasons, will thrive; others, for different but often obvious reasons, will fail. All who persist in their careers will need additional knowledge, assistance and guidance as the years pass. We must prepare teachers who see their early experiences in teaching as just that: early experiences preparing them for a life-long career of teaching and learning. We need internships and induction models based on this premise. We need faculty who see their obligations to students extending beyond campus programs.

Preparation programs, whatever their duration, must be such that students perceive themselves and their faculty as lifelong learners, persons continually open to new learning. Graduates must be aware that what they learn for situation A may not fit situation B, just as good professors realize they must somewhat fashion themselves anew with each new group. We expect such professors to prepare their students so they see themselves as continual learners, as individuals striving to grow and improve. Teachers and their professors must be students all their lives. These are not merely statements of ideals. They are goals that can be concretely demonstrated in first-rate teacher preparation curricula.

## THE CHALLENGE TO LEAD

If there is any one characteristic of the education professoriate that discourages us it is the lack of leadership on the part of many of our colleagues. Most professors of teaching are far more reactors than interveners in the educational scene. It is for this reason that college of education faculty respond very slowly to changing conditions in the schools and society.

It is axiomatic that professional schools have lower status in the pecking order of universities. Education is not alone in its sometimes beleaguered status. Such knowledge ought neither to discourage nor intimidate professors of teaching. It has long been so; it will probably long remain so. It is unlikely that even major increases in SAT or ACT scores of education students, international awards for educational research, higher salaries for teachers, or any other change will significantly after the perceptions held by some. Prejudices die hard.

Because we are slow and reluctant to alter practices, the criticism of schools of education will persist. We recognize that the denigration of education will not be significantly mitigated in our lifetimes. Some criticisms are valid; most fall into the adage describing people living in glass houses. We also acknowledge that on some campuses such attacks are becoming less important and relations between educators and other disciplines are improving.

A frequently voiced prejudice revolves around the quality of students of education. Education professors have been tarnished by the quality of students admitted into schools of education. The admission standards of schools of education, for what is at the heart of an academic calling, have been too low. This assessment in no way disparages the many talented and committed persons who have graduated from schools of education. Furthermore, the level of performance expected of students is an equally powerful factor in assessing student quality. Such norms are clearly the responsibility of a faculty.

The powerful imagery of low admission criteria has been challenged in recent years and is being reversed. Recent trends indicate that education students on many campuses are now at or above the norms for campuses as a whole. This was not the case for decades, as test data have revealed. A turn-around appears to be taking place and it is one we applaud. This does not mean that snide comments about students in schools of education will disappear. We repeat: prejudices die hard.

Education professors must be champions of increased quality in the competition for students without yielding on providing access to the teaching profession. Schools of education must demonstrate a commitment to equity followed by rigorous expectations of performance. In many ways, professors of education must demonstrate the highest ideals of public education. To those who do not grapple with the dilemmas inherent in championing quality while, at the same time, defending access, the decisions faced by education professors will be difficult to understand. We side with the view that providing access along with high expectations is an attainable goal; difficult, but not impossible. To argue otherwise would mock the highest aspirations of a democratic society.

In respect to scholarly productivity, contributors to this volume have underscored that the research output of education faculty is on a par with that of faculty in other disciplines. We need strengthening in this arena, but the issue is campuswide rather than exclusively in schools of education. It is clear that educational research can play a significant role in altering schooling practices. If these trends continue, our knowledge of and pride in our accomplishments count more than what may be said by some. While we acknowledge our weaknesses, we will not give any quarter with respect to our strengths.

We urge the education professoriate to seize upon its strengths, to celebrate its work, and to stimulate others in its ranks to achieve more. The work of schools of education is *education*, not the mimicry of other disciplines or professional schools. Education faculty, we believe, must take the initiative in asserting the validity of their work. Our work is too important to society to squander time on what others think of us and how we might change their thinking or biases.

More importantly, we make a strong claim for what is necessary in the preparation of teachers. Like any profession, we are no doubt blind to some failings. The opinions and advice of responsible critics are welcome. But we will not accept uninformed or irrational attacks. In the past, we have yielded too easily to attacks on the importance of professional, pedagogical skills.

Foretelling the future is not difficult when done with a broad brush. Our discussion, research, and debates reflect problems, issues, and characteristics of the education professoriate as they have existed for decades. It is obvious that these patterns of behavior will continue with but minor variations into the future. This prognosis is readily apparent from Schwebel's meta-view of forces that drive education, and the deep roots of our calling as described by Hazlett and Allison.

The future of teacher education can be more dynamic and positive than the weak and mediocre colleagues in our midst apparently wish. Whatever the reasons some individuals have for standing pat, we stand with those responding to the reform movement and to the ideals of our calling. Those implementing needed reforms are the best hope for strengthened and revitalized schools of education. They are persons with whom we share a cautious optimism regarding the future.

We must become increasingly effective in the work the best of us do well: model good teaching; engage in scholarship; work closely with the field; and mentor young faculty into the fullness of academic life. Done well, these activities are the proper calling of the professors of teaching.

## REFERENCES

Gideonse, H. D. (1987). The moral obligations and implications of clinical fidelity for teacher education. *Journal of Thought, 22* (2), 41–46.

Lederman, D. (1987). Act to reform schools, chiefs of 37 colleges urge all presidents. *Chronicle of Higher Education, 34* (4), pp. 1, 22–23.

Schaefer, R. J. (1967). *The school as a center of inquiry,* (John Dewey Society Lectureship Series, No. 9). New York: Harper.

Sizer, T. R., & Powell, A. G. (1969). Changing conceptions of the professors of education. In J. S. Counelis (Ed.), *To be a Phoenix: The education professoriate* (pp. 61–76). Bloomington, Ind.: Phi Delta Kappa.

# BIBLIOGRAPHY

*Most of the following references are specific to the education professoriate. Also included are some works that treat the professoriate generically.*

Adams, R., & Hord, S. (1985, October). *A workshop on the professoriate.* Paper presented at the annual meeting of the Teacher Education Council of State Colleges and Universities, St. Louis, Mo.

Allison, C. (1983). The University of Tennessee faculty controversy of 1923. *Proceedings of the Thirty-third Annual Meeting of the Southwestern Philosophy of Education Society, 33*, 107–113.

_____ (1983). Training Dixie's teachers: The University of Tennessee's Summer Normal Institutes. *Journal of Thought, 18*(3), 27–36.

_____ (1984). The summer school of the South. *Proceedings of the Thirty-fourth Annual Meeting of the Southwestern Philosophy of Education Society, 34*, 194–201.

_____ (1985), November). *The country life movement in Tennessee: Educationists and rural reform.* Paper presented at the Meeting of the History of Education Society, Atlanta.

Altbach, P. (Ed.). (1977). The academic profession in comparative perspective (Special Issue). *Higher Education, 6*, 131–276.

American Association of Colleges for Teacher Education. (1987). *Teaching and teachers: Facts and figures.* Washington, D.C.: American Association of Colleges for Teacher Education.

Anderson, J. (1984). Toward a history and bibliography of the Afro-American doctorate and professoriate in education, 1896 to 1980. In A. Bagley (Ed.), *The Black education professoriate.* Minneapolis: Society of Professors of Education, College of Education, University of Minnesota.

Applied Systems Institute, Inc. (1985). *Tomorrow's teachers* (rev. ed.). Washington, D.C.: U. S. Department of Education.

Arends, R., Murphy, J., & Christensen, P. (1986). Faculty development for teacher educators. *Journal of Teacher Education, 37*(5), 17–23.

Bagley, A. (Ed.). (1975). *The professor of education: An assessment of conditions.* Minneapolis: Society of Professors of Education, College of Education, University of Minnesota.

Baldwin, R., & Blackburn, R. (1983). The condition of the professoriate: The variables and the data bases. *New directions for institutional research, 40,* 15–27.

Bell, M., & Morsink, C. (1986). Quality and equity in the preparation of black teachers. *Journal of Teacher Education, 37* (2), 10–15.

Berliner, D. C. (1983). Special issue: Research on teaching. *Educational Psychologist, 18.*

_____ (1984, October). *Contemporary teacher education: Timidity, lack of vision and ignorance.* Paper presented at the meeting of the National Academy of Education, Berkeley, Calif.

Bestor, A. (1985). *Educational wastelands: The retreat from learning* (2nd. ed.). Champaign, Ill.: University of Illinois Press.

Blackburn, R., & Lawrence, J. (1986). Aging and the quality of faculty job performance. *Review of Educational Research, 56* (3), 265–90.

Bledstein, B. (1976). *The culture of professionalism: The middle class and the development of higher education in America.* New York: W. W. Norton & Co.

Bok, D. (1986). *Higher learning.* Cambridge, Mass.: Harvard University Press.

Borrowman, M. (1956). *The liberal and technical in teacher education.* New York: Teachers College Bureau of Publications.

_____ (1965). (Ed.). *Teacher education in America: A documentary history.* New York: Teachers College Press.

_____ (1975). About professors of education. In A. Bagley (Ed.), *The professor of education: An assessment of conditions.* Minneapolis: Society of Professors of Education, College of Education, University of Minnesota.

Brittingham, B. (1986). Faculty development in teacher education: An agenda. *Journal of Teacher Education, 37* (5), 2–5.

Brooks, M., & German, K. (1983). *Meeting the challenges: Developing faculty careers* (Research Report No. 3). Washington, D.C.: Association for the Study of Higher Education. (ERIC Document Reproduction Service No. ED 232 516.)

Broudy, H. (1980, 1981). What do professors of education profess? *Educational Forum, 44,* 441–51. (Discussion: 45, 404–10.)

Browne, J. (1979). *Teachers of teachers.* Sevenoaks, England: Hodder and Soughton.

Bullough, R., Jr. (1982). Professional schizophrenia: Teacher education in confusion. *Contemporary Education, 53,* 207–12.

Byram, H. (1983). *Some problems in the provision of professional education for college teachers.* New York: Teachers College, The Rumford Press.

Cadenhead, K. (1985). Is substantive change in teacher education possible? *Journal of Teacher Education, 36* (4), 17–20.

Cahn, S. (1986). *Saints and scamps: Ethics in academia.* Totowa, N.J.: Rowman and Littlefield.

Cain, M. (1975). Affirmative action, women, and the education professoriate. In A. Bagley (Ed.), *The professor of education: An assessment of conditions.* Minneapolis: Society of Professors of Education, College of Education, University of Minnesota.

Campbell, R., & Newell, L. (1973). *A study of professors of educational administration.* Columbus, Ohio: University Council for Educational Administration.

Carnegie Forum on Education and Economy. (1985). *A nation prepared: Teachers for the 21st century.* New York: The Carnegie Forum.

Carter, H. (1981) *Teacher educators: A descriptive study.* University of Texas, Research and Development Center for Teacher Education. (ERIC Document Reproduction Service No. ED 255 354.)

_____ (1984). Teachers of teachers. In L. Katz & J. Raths (Eds.), *Advances in teacher education,* (Vol. 1) Norwood, N.J.: Ablex Publishing Corp.

Case, C., & Matthes, W. (1985). *Colleges of education: Perspectives on their future* (text ed.). Berkeley, Calif.: McCutchan Publishing Corp.

Clark, B. (1987). *The academic life: Small worlds, different worlds.* Princeton, N.J.: The Carnegie Foundation for the Advancement of Teaching.

Clark, D. (1978). *Research and development productivity in educational organizations* (Occasional Paper No. 41). Columbus, Ohio: National Center for Research in Vocational Education, The Ohio State University.

Clear, D. (1983). Malpractice in teacher education: The impossible becomes increasingly possible. *Journal of Teacher Education, 34* (3), 10–24.

Conant, J. B. (1963). *The education of American teachers.* New York: McGraw-Hill Book Co., Inc.

Counelis, J. (Ed.). (1969). *To be a Phoenix: The education professoriate.* Blooming-ton, Ind.: Phi Delta Kappa.

Cyphert, F., & Spaights, E. (1964). *An analysis and projection of research in teacher education.* (ERIC Document Reproduction Service No. ED 003 399.)

Denmark, G., & Nutter, N. (1984). The case for extended programs of initial teacher preparation. In L. Katz & J. Raths (Eds.), *Advances in teacher education* (pp. 204–46). Norwood, N.J.: Ablex Publishing Corp.

Denton, J., Tsai, C-Y., & Cloud, C. (1986). Productivity of faculty in higher education institutions. *Journal of Teacher Education, 37* (5), 12–16.

Ducharme, E. (1985). Establishing the place of teacher education in the uni-versity. *Journal of Teacher Education, 36* (4), 8–11.

———— (1985). Teacher educators: Description and analysis. In J. Raths & L. Katz (Eds.), *Advances in teacher education,* (Vol. 2). Norwood, N. J.: Ablex Publishing Corp.

———— (1986). Teacher educators: What do we know? *ERIC Digest 15.* Wash-ington D. C.: ERIC Clearinghouse on Teacher Education. (ERIC Doc-ument Reproduction Service No. ED 279 642.)

———— (1987). Developing existing teacher education faculty. In C. Magrath & R. Egbert (Eds.), *Strengthening teacher education: The challenges to college and university leaders.* San Francisco: Jossey-Bass Publishers.

———— & Agne, R. (1982). The education professoriate: A research-based per-spective. *Journal of Teacher Education, 33* (6), 30–36.

———— (1987). Professors of education: Beasts of burden, facilitators, or aca-demicians. *Journal of Human Behavior and Learning, 4,* 1–9.

Emans, R. (1982). Role of professors of method in educational research. *Jour-nal of Teacher Education, 33* (4), 16–21.

Esch, M. (1983). Educational research productivity of institutions of higher education. *American Educational Research Journal, 20,* 5–12.

Evertson, C., Hawley, W., & Zoltnik, M. (1984). *The characteristics of effective teacher preparation programs: Review of research.* Nashville, Tenn.: Vander-bilt University, Peabody Center for Effective Teaching.

Foundations of teacher education. (1982). (Symposium). *Journal of Teacher Education, 33* (3), 1–8,

Finkelstein, B. (1982). Technicians, mandarians, and witnesses: Searching for professional understanding. *Journal of Teacher Education, 33* (3), 25–27.

Fuller, F., & Bown, O. (1975). Becoming a teacher. In K. Ryan (Ed.), *Teacher education* (74th Yearbook of the National Society for the Study of Education) (Part 2, pp. 25–52). Chicago: University of Chicago Press.

Gideonse, H. (1983). *In search of more effective service.* Cincinnati, Ohio: Rosenthal.

_____ (1987). The moral obligations and implications of clinical fidelity for teacher education. *Journal of Thought, 22* (2), 41–46.

_____ & Joseph, E. (1984). *Increasing research capacity in schools of education: A policy inquiry and dialogue.* Cincinnati, Ohio: Fleuron Press.

Gore, J. (1981). Collegial ambience: Its necessity in teacher education. *Journal of Teacher Education, 32,* 37–9.

Graham, P. (1987). Black teachers: A drastically scarce resource. *Phi Delta Kappan, 68* (8), 598–605.

Guba, E., & Clark D. (1978). Levels of R & D productivity in schools of education. *Educational Researcher, 7* (5), 3–9.

Haberman, M., & Stinnett, T. (1973). *Teacher education and the new profession of teaching.* Berkeley, Calif.: McCutchan Publishing Corp.

Highet, G. (1976). *The immortal profession: The joys of teaching and learning.* New York: Weybright and Talley.

Hilliard, F. (Ed.). (1971). *Teaching the teachers: Trends in teacher education.* London: George Allen and Unwin Ltd.

Holmes Group. (1985). *Tomorrow's teachers: A report of the Holmes Group.* East Lansing, Mich.: The Holmes Group.

Howsam, R., Corrigan, D., Denemark, G., & Nash, R. (1976). *Educating a profession.* Washington, D.C.: American Association of Colleges for Teacher Education.

Imig, D. G., & Imig, D. R. (1987). Strengthening and maintaining the pool of qualified teachers. In C. Magrath & R. Egbert (Eds.), *Strengthening teacher education: The challenges to college and university leaders.* San Francisco: Jossey-Bass Publishers.

Jackson, P. (1975). Divided we stand: Observations on the internal organization of the education professoriate. In A. Bagley (Ed.), *The professor of education: An assessment of conditions*. Minneapolis: Society of Professors of Education, College of Education, University of Minnesota.

Jarvis, P. (1983). *Professional education*. London: Croom Helm.

Johanningmeier, E. (Ed.). (1978). *Science of education and the education professoriate*. Minneapolis: Society of Professors of Education, College of Education, University of Minnesota.

Johanningmeier, E., & Johnson, H., Jr. (1975). The education professoriate: A historical consideration of its work and growth. In A. Bagley (Ed.), *The professor of education: An assessment of conditions*. Minneapolis: Society of Professors of Education, College of Education, University of Minnesota.

Johnson, H., Jr., & Johanningmeier, E. (1972). *Teachers for the prairie*. Urbana Ill.: University of Illinois Press.

Joyce, B., & Clift, R. (1984). The Phoenix agenda: Essential reform in teacher education. *Educational Researcher, 13*, 5–19.

Judge, H. (1982). *American graduate schools of education: A view from abroad*. New York: The Ford Foundation.

Katz, M. (1966). From theory to survey in graduate schools of education. *Journal of Higher Education, 36*, 325–334.

Katz, L., & Raths, J. (Eds.). (1984). *Advances in teacher education* (Vol. 1). Norwood, N.J.: Ablex Publishing Corp.

Katz, L. G., Raths, J. D., Irving, J., Kurachi, A., Mohanty, C., & Soni, M. (1982, March). *Reputations of teacher educators among members of their role–set*. Paper presented at the Annual Meeting of the American Educational Research Association, New York. (ERIC Document Reproduction Service, ED 213 486.)

Kluender, M. (1984). Teacher education programs in the 1980s: Some characteristics. *Journal of Teacher Education, 35* (4), 33–35.

Koerner, J. (1963). *The miseducation of American teachers*. Boston: Houghton Mifflin Company.

Ladd, E. (1979). The work experience of American college professors: Some data and an argument. *Current issues in higher education; 1979* [The Jossey-Bass series in higher education] (pp. 3–13). San Francisco: Jossey-Bass Publishers.

_____ Jr., & Lipset, S. M. (1975). The divided academy: Professors and politics [Carnegie Commission of Higher Education]. New York: McGraw-Hill Book Company.

Lanier, J. (1984). The preservice teacher education improvement project: A critical review. *Journal of Teacher Education, 35* (4) 24–28.

_____ & Little, J. (1986). Research on teacher education. In M. Wittrock (Ed.), *Handbook of research on teaching* (3rd ed.). New York: Macmillan Company.

Lasley, T. (Ed.). (1986). *The dynamics of change in teacher education* (Vol. 1, Monograph No. 5). Washington, D.C.: American Association of Colleges for Teacher Education. (ERIC Document Reproduction Service No. ED 272 512.)

_____ (1986). *Issues in teacher education* (Vol. 2, Monograph No. 6). Washington, D.C.: American Association of Colleges for Teacher Education. (ERIC Document Reproduction Service No. ED 272 513.)

Lederman, D. (1987). Act to reform schools, chiefs of 37 colleges urge all presidents. *Chronicle of Higher Education, 34* (4), pp. 1, 22–23.

Lopez, T. R., & Balzar, D. M. (1984). Possibilities for the scholarly life in colleges of education. In D. Tavel (Ed.), *Modern educational controversies* (p. 318). Lanham, Md.: University of America Press.

Lortie, D. (1975). *Schoolteacher: A sociological study.* Chicago: University of Chicago Press.

Mager, G., & Myers, B. (1983). *Developing a career in the academy.* Minneapolis: Society of Professors of Education, College of Education, University of Minnesota.

Magrath, C., & Egbert, R. (Eds.). (1987). *Strengthening teacher education: The challenges to college and university leaders.* San Francisco: Jossey-Bass Publishers.

Marsicano, H. (1981). *Role of mentors in developing careers: Do women need mentors?* Paper presented at the West Virginia University Council on Women's Concerns—A Conference on Women's Career Management: Challenges and Decision. (ERIC Document Reproduction Service No. ED 203 132.)

Mitra, S. K. (1974). A brief note on American education research. *American Educational Research Journal, 11,* 41–47.

Myers, B., & Mager, G. (1980). *The emerging professoriate: A study of how new professors spend their time.* (ERIC Document Reproduction Service No. ED 220 429.)

National Commission for Excellence in Teacher Education. (1985). *A call for change in teacher education*. Washington: American Association of Colleges for Teacher Education.

Nelson, W. (1981). *Renewal of the teacher-scholar: Faculty development in the liberal arts college* (p. 7). Washington, D.C.: Association of American Colleges. (ERIC Document Reproduction Service No. ED 215 602.)

Nolan, J. (1985). Potential obstacles to internal reform in teacher education: Findings from a case study. *Journal of Teacher Education, 36* (4), 12–16.

Oftedahl, J., & Kilgore, A. (no date). *A study of the congruence of goals and activities of methods courses between professors and students*. Unpublished manuscript, University of Nebraska-Lincoln, Center for Curriculum and Instruction, Teachers College.

Peseau, B. A. (1982). Developing an adequate resource base for teacher education. *Journal of Teacher Education, 33* (4), 13–15.

Peseau, B. A., & Orr, P. G. (1980). The outrageous underfunding of teacher education. *Phi Delta Kappan, 62* (2), 100–02.

Pickle, J. (1981). Perspectives of educators across clinical and scholarly/scientific work settings. *College Student Journal, 17,* 190–95.

Powell, A. (1980). *The uncertain profession: Harvard and the search for educational authority*. Cambridge, Mass.: Harvard University Press.

Raths, J. (1985). *A profile of methods instructors in teacher education*. Washington, D.C.: American Association of Colleges for Teacher Education. (ERIC Document Reproduction Service No. SP 026 037.)

_____ & Katz, L. (1985). *Advances in teacher education* (Vol. 2). Norwood, NJ: Ablex Publishing Corp.

_____ & Katz, L. (Eds.). (1982). The best of intentions for the education of teachers. *Journal of Education for Teaching, 8,* 275–83.

_____ & Ruchkin, J. (1984, February) *Contexts affecting methods instruction in selected teacher education institutions*. Paper presented at the Annual Meeting of the American Association of Colleges for Teacher Education, San Antonio. (ERIC Document Reproduction Service No. ED 240 081.)

Reagan, C. (1975). Education professoriate: The concept, some problems and some proposals. In A. Bagley (Ed.), *The professor of education: An assessment of conditions*. Minneapolis: Society of Professors of Education, College of Education, University of Minnesota.

Rhodes, D., & Eisele, C. (1986, February). *Preparing teachers for the twentieth century: Lessons from an unmet challenge of the past.* Paper presented at the annual meeting of the Association of Teacher Educators, Atlanta, Ga.

Rich, J. (Ed.). (1984). *Professional ethics and the education professor.* Minneapolis: Society of Professors of Education, College of Education, University of Minnesota.

Roemer, R., & Martinello, M. (1982). Divisions in the educational professoriate and the future of professional education. *Educational Studies, 13,* 203–23.

Russell, J. (1965). A summary of some of the difficulties connected with the making of a teachers college. In M. E. Borrowman (Ed.), *Teacher education in America: A documentary history* (pp. 208–17). New York: Teachers College Press.

Ryan, K. (Ed.). (1975). *Teacher education* (74th yearbook of the National Society for the Study of Education) Pt. 2. Chicago: Distributed by University of Chicago Press.

Schein, E. (1972). *Professional education: Some new directions.* New York: McGraw-Hill Book Company.

Schneider, B., & Raths, J. (1983). Teacher educators: Do they have a place in research oriented universities? *The High School Journal, 66,* 70–82.

Schwab, J. J. (1978). The practical: A language for curriculum. In I Westbury & N. J. Wilkof(Eds.), *Science, curriculum and liberal education: Selected essays,* (pp. 287–321). Chicago: University of Chicago Press.

Schwebel, M. (1982). Research productivity of education faculty: A comparative study. *Educational Studies, 13,* 224–39.

Schwebel, M. (1985). The clash of cultures of academe: The university and the education faculty. *Journal of Teacher Education, 36* (4), 2–7.

Sizer, T., & Powell, A. (1969). Changing conceptions of the professor of education. In J. Counelis (Ed.), *To be a Phoenix: The education professoriate* (pp. 61–76). Bloomington, Ind.: Phi Delta Kappa.

Spillane, R. (1982). Some unfortunate assumptions. *Phi Delta Kappan, 64* (1), 2.

Stewart, D. (1985). Materials on the education professoriate in the ERIC database. *Journal of Teacher Education, 37* (5), 24–26.

Troyer, M. (1986). A synthesis of research on the characteristics of teacher educators. *Journal of Teacher Education, 37* (5), 6–11.

Tucker, S. B. (1984). Increasing the research capacity of schools of education: A policy inquiry, March, 1981. In H. Gideonse & E. Joseph (Eds.), *Increasing research capacity in schools of education: A policy inquiry and dialogue* (pp. 7–28). Cincinnati: Fleuron Press.

Weidman, C. S., & Weidman, J. C. (1975). Professors of education: Some social and occupational characteristics. In A. Bagley (Ed.), *The professor of education: An assessment of conditions* (pp. 87–101). Minneapolis: Society of Professors of Education, College of Education, University of Minnesota.

Wisniewski, R. (1983). *Too many schools of education? Too little scholarship?* Minneapolis: Society of Professors of Education, College of Education, University of Minnesota.

_____ (1984). The scholarly ethos in schools of education. *Journal of Teacher Education, 35* (3), 2–8.

_____ (1986). The ideal professor of education. *Phi Delta Kappan, 68* (4), 288–92.

Wittrock, M. (Ed.). (1986). *Handbook of research on teaching* (3rd ed.). New York: Macmillan & Company.